The Psychology of Super-Conscious Mind

By the same author

Metaphysical Realities in Psychology and Management: A Sacred Path to Intutive Awareness (Concept, 2011)

Management Through Interpersonal Relationships (Jaico, 2007)

About the Author

M B Sharan, Ph.D. is currently Senior Professor of Psychology at IIT Patna. He is Ex-Professor of Psychology, Department of Humanities & Social Sciences, IIT, Kharagpur where he taught psychology and management courses to undergraduate and postgraduate students for more than three decades. During this period, he headed the Department twice and served on various committees of the IIT, UGC, UPSC, etc. and presented many papers at national and international conferences. He started his career as a Lecturer in Psychology in Patna and Bhagalpur Universities. After retirement from IIT service in 2005, he served as Dean (Academic) and Principal at RIMS, Rourkela and as Emeritus Professor at PIET, Rourkela till 2009. He has been writing books and publishing articles in national and international journals. He was president of the National Academy of Psychology for the year 2006-07. His biography is published in "Who's Who in the World" (8th edition).

The Psychology of Super-Conscious Mind

An Inward Journey for Enlightened Living

by

M.B. Sharan, Ph.D.

Foreword by

David Mutchler, Ph.D

CONCEPT PUBLISHING COMPANY PVT. LTD.
NEW DELHI-110059

ISBN-13 : 978-93-5125-027-2

First Published 2014

Published and Printed by

Concept
Since 1974

Concept Publishing Company Pvt. Ltd.
A/15-16, Commercial Block, Mohan Garden
New Delhi-110059 (India)
T: 25351460, 25351794, *F*: 091-11-25357109
E: publishing@conceptpub.com, W: www.conceptpub.com
Editorial Office: H-13, Bali Nagar, New Delhi-110 015, India.

Cataloging in Publication Data--*Courtesy:* D.K. Agencies (P) Ltd. <docinfo@dkagencies.com>

Sharan, M. B. (Mithila Bihari), 1943-
The psychology of super-conscious mind : an inward journey for enlightened living/ by M.B. Sharan ; foreword by David Mutchler.
p. cm.
Includes bibliographical references and index.
ISBN 9789351250272

1. Success--Psychological aspects. 2. Yoga. 3. Spirituality. 4. Psychology. I. Title.

DDC 158.1 23

Dedicated to

The Association for Research and Enlightenment (A.R.E.)
(Founded by Edgar Cayce)
For
Teaching the world
How to dig deeper than the
subconscious and unconscious mind
And
See a vast vista of the Super-Conscious Mind
Merged with the Universe and its Creator

What Others Say About the Book

That is a great title. I am so proud of you and your accomplishments. Congratulations.

Henry Reed, Ph.D.
Professor of Transpersonal Studies, Atlantic University
Director, Edgar Cayce Institute for Intuitive Studies

"The Psychology of Super-Conscious Mind" authored by a senior psychologist who taught students of the first IIT of this country nearly forty years, supervised a number of doctoral thesis, and have mentored brightest young men of the nation, is a description of a long journey one may decide to take for shaping of mind, body up to a level of super spiritual consciousness, a capacity of freeing individual of worldly difficulties and constraints and keeping thriving by achieving best of the creativity for oneself and the larger society. The book could serve as a practical guide to enrich oneself.

Janak Pandey, Ph.D.
Vice-Chancellor
Central University of Bihar, Patna, Bihar, India

I consider it a great privilege and honour to get this opportunity to write a few lines about the book, ***"The Psychology of Super-Conscious Mind"****, by*

Professor M.B. Sharan. Adding to the recent series of books written by Professor Sharan, this one further brings out the essence of value-based psychology. Through nine chapters that are written in a very readable style, the author points attention to the importance of some basic concepts of Indian psychology. These ideas provide an alternative frame for the interpretation and comprehension of psychological processes and phenomena that are familiar to those in the field of contemporary psychology. The themes discussed in the book include concepts ranging from spirituality and God to the contributions made by the Tatas to Indian life. In short, the book presents thought-provoking ideas laid out in simple language, and is definitely worth reading.

Lilavati Krishnan, Ph.D.
Professor, Dept. of Humanities & Social Sciences
IIT Kanpur, U.P., India

The present volume ventures to enlarge the scope of mental sciences by addressing questions of life and existence in a relative less explored framework. Confined to a materialist, reductionistic and mechanical framework psychological scholarship has so far been primarily dedicated to the reality at a surface level in a trivial fashion. It has ignored the larger picture and failed in acknowledging a wide range of phenomena which have potential to influence human lives in significant ways. Professor Sharan has been sincerely pursuing inquiry into the realm of metaphysical and consciousness related issues. The present work is culmination of Prof. Sharan's critical and systematic engagement with issues which are meta-theoretical and have profound implications for conceptualizing the quest for being and becoming. Succinct in presentation and comprehensive in scope the volume stimulates our thinking and demands revisiting some of the basic and taken for granted premises of the science of psychology. The community of psychologists is obliged to Prof. Sharan for drawing attention to some of the important but neglected issues. It's a worth reading text for the scholars of Psychology, Philosophy and other related disciplines.

Girishwar Misra, Ph.D.
Dean Research (Humanities & Social Sciences)
Professor of Psychology, Delhi University, Delhi, India

In simple and convincing tone, Prof. Sharan shows us the ways to be a spiritual person. A spiritual life can be adopted by practising yoga and meditation, involving in philanthropic activities, realizing the self, expressing love, living in present, getting associated with the sacred, praying to God, and experiencing His bliss.

Damodar Suar, Ph.D.
Professor, Department of Humanities and Social Sciences
IIT Kharagpur, West Bengal, India

Foreword

Increasingly, we live in an age of specialization and specialists. We no longer have just "medical doctors." We have internists, dermatologists, cardiologists, endocrinologists, oncologists, haematologists, rheumatologists, obstetricians, ophthalmologists, psychiatrists, and so many more.

Nor do we have simply "engineers." Now there are civil engineers, industrial engineers, electrical engineers, computer hardware engineers, traffic engineers, health and safety engineers, marine engineers, and so on.

Nor do we have simply "world religions," such as Hinduism and Christianity. Hinduism, for example, has several denominations: Vaishnavism, Saivism, Shaktism, Smartism, and Shrautaism. Christianity is divided into Catholic, Orthodox, and Protestant, with Protestants alone having over 30,000 denominations.

There is clearly a positive outcome in this regard: specific diseases can now receive highly specific treatments; various arenas in life require certain engineering specialists to address their challenges; and the many religions on the planet minister to different peoples with differing needs.

However, there is clearly a downside to this age of extreme specialization: it tends to fractionalize and divide a world of peoples who, in truth, are all One. In this context, people call the same thing by different names. For example, all that exists is derived from a single source of divine energy. Traditional religions believe this source of energy is the Supreme Being they worship: Jehovah in Christianity,

Brahman in Hinduism, and Allah in Islam. In non-traditional religions, and in the secular world in general, this energy is often referred to as the universe, the source, the force, or reality. But there is only one world. So, in fact, these various names all describe the same thing. Yet people cling to their own beliefs and are willing to fight to defend them, and thus the world is fractionalized.

It is indeed refreshing when minds come along that have the ability to reintegrate that which seems separate but, in fact, is all One. Such thinkers are holistic in their approach, and are able to address multiple subjects while still knowing that they are all interrelated and woven together in an intricate web of existence.

Professor M.B. Sharan is a fine example of such a person. He is a scholar in many disciplines, yet he exhibits a deep appreciation and respect for the intrinsic oneness that exists in a world of plurality.

Here he ties together in one book his understanding of the human mind and behaviour, social transformation and *yoga*, spiritual development and counselling for college students, the success of Tatas, the concept of God, the power of prayer and meditation, the source of intuitive knowledge, the psychodynamics of miracles, and the ultimate purpose of human life: spiritual consciousness.

In our world of specialization, one might conclude that these are divergent topics to be addressed only by those who specialize in each of them. Yet one cannot read Dr. Sharan's work without soon understanding that these various topics emanate from One mind, from a truly holistic thinker. This being true, readers also have the unique opportunity to experience his wisdom about the interconnected nature of all reality.

Dr. David Mutchler.
www.drdavidmutchler.com
Author of:
Beyond the Ego
Lessons for Living Beyond the Ego
Non-Judgment Day Is Coming : Are You Ready?
Fourteen Inches to Peace

Acknowledgements

About two years back when my previous book, *Metaphysical Realities in Psychology and Management* came out, I was happy to learn that many persons liked that book. This was the motivating force working in my mind to write some more articles related to spirituality. This way, I went on writing and getting them published in the online magazine, Intuitive-Connections Network published by Atlantic University. Since this book is a collection of these articles, my first thanks go to the Editor of the magazine, Dr. Henry Reed for appreciating and publishing my articles quickly.

While writing these articles, I must say that it was something like walking on a spiritual path under the guidance of my Soul and getting newer and newer experiences. Today, when my book, *The Psychology of Super-Conscious Mind* is coming out as a collection of those articles, I must express my gratitude to my Soul, my Higher Self, and my God.

Nobody can write a book, unless he or she is given an opportunity and environment to do so. For this reason, I am thankful to Prof. Anil K. Bhowmick, Director, IIT Patna and Prof. A.T. Khan, Ex-Dean of Faculty Affairs, IIT Patna for giving me this opportunity and environment by putting me in active service of doing teaching and research work in this great Institute as I was doing in IIT, Kharagpur before my retirement. I am really feeling young, energetic, and elevated.

For writing a book, the author is supposed to consult a number of books, journals, and other published and unpublished articles available on Internet. I also have done the same thing. I am, therefore, indebted to all those authors and writers—published or unpublished ones—for giving me their ideas and quoting them in my book. In this process, it is possible; I might have missed some names which I could not get for listing them in References and Bibliographies. I apologize to them.

When I was going through some books by foreign authors, I could get a chance to read the book, *Beyond the Ego* by Dr. David Mutchler. I got so much impressed by this book that I decided to approach him for writing the Foreword to my book. He was so nice with me that after going through the manuscript he wrote the Foreword and sent it to me within a fortnight. For this, I shall remain grateful to him forever.

There are some of my professional colleagues, well-known in the field of Psychology for their research, publications, and holding high positions, have also gone through the manuscript of my book on my request and have expressed their views. I am thankful to each one of them for taking time and going through the manuscript. All their views are printed in the book under the heading: "What Others Say About The Book".

I am also thankful to Miss Sadeqa Ghazal, Research Scholar in English, School of Humanities & Social Sciences, IIT Patna for going through the manuscript and suggesting corrections and Mr. M. Rahman, Junior Assistant, IIT Patna for typing and setting the materials for printing.

Finally, my affectionate thanks go to my soul mate, Savita Sharan for her sacrifice, tolerance, and patient love which have enabled me to reach this level where I am today.

Contents

Introduction

DIFFERENT LAYERS OF THE HUMAN MIND

Human mind, as a whole, is one. However, from functional viewpoint, there are three different layers—conscious, subconscious, and unconscious. The first layer, known as the conscious mind, houses our brain and emotions with which we perform our regular activities with the help of five sense organs and five organs of action. When we are doing something, talking to someone, or concentrating, we make use of this mind. This part of the mind, however, is the tip of an ice berg – one-tenth of the whole mind. The remaining part (nine-tenth) is below, which we cannot see. Psychologists, particularly Freud and Jung, have pointed out that this remaining part consists of two different layers – subconscious and unconscious minds. When the conscious mind is active, the subconscious mind starts its own processing and recording its all activities in terms of memories. As a result, the conscious mind is able to recall these materials as and when needed. This way, the subconscious mind helps the conscious mind to remember, and holds a major responsibility of keeping the records in terms of short-term and long-term memories. Not only that, it also keeps the physical body properly coordinated by adjusting hormone levels, respiration and heartbeats, digestions, and other autonomic functions. Thus, the subconscious mind plays a vital role in the life of a person. Even when our conscious is not active or taking rest during sleep, it is functioning. Some persons say that if we want to attract something with good intention, we need to create a clear pattern of that item in the subconscious mind. Then, automatically, the subconscious mind creates a magnetic force in the environment at different levels which paves the way to reach that item. The third layer of the unconscious mind is known as "forgotten" mind. It is like a store house in which all unsatisfied desires, conflicts, frustrations, and anxieties are repressed. These painful repressed memories manifest themselves through symptoms, dreams, and neurotic and psychotic behaviours. Though it has a record of all the past experiences and influences our personality in various ways, they cannot be recalled easily by the conscious mind. Some persons think that it is also a reservoir of the entire subliminal psychic contents as well as the wisdom and experiences of uncounted centuries. Therefore, we need to learn how to be guided by these transcendent truths. For this reason, Jung has an edge over Freud so far unconscious mind is concerned.

THE SOUL'S MIND: SUPER-CONSCIOUS MIND

We should not be misguided by different functions of the conscious, subconscious, and unconscious minds because they work together as "one mind". They communicate with each other instantly, and they are accessible to us in some way. We, therefore, need to develop such a mind which can perceive and judge things rightly all the time, and can suggest the right path to follow so that we can achieve love, peace, and harmony in our life. Today, many persons say that it is possible to develop such a mind known as "Super-Conscious Mind". This is not a separate layer of the mind but using the whole "one mind" to function in such a way that it becomes the Soul's Mind. In reality, every human mind is the Soul's mind because it cannot function without being illuminated by the Soul. As *Vedanta* says, mind is an internal instrument like a mirror which does not have the built-in characteristic of consciousness. Therefore, consciousness has to be put in it by the Soul as it is being put in other parts of the body to function. Thus, when the mind is illuminated, it starts functioning. But its proper functioning depends on how much it is illuminated. If it is not neat and clean, it cannot be illuminated fully. But if it is, it can absorb the lights fully and can perceive the world in right perspective. Up-till-now, many of us are working with "ordinary" state of mind, and have ordinary perceptions including illusions and hallucinations. But some are working with "extended" state of mind, and have some extra-sensory perceptions as well like telepathy and precognition. On the other hand, there are some persons like *yogis* and sages who are working with a "higher" state of mind and have extraordinary perceptions. Such a state of mind is known as Super-Conscious Mind or Universal Mind. Therefore, it has been rightly said that there are no miracles for *yogis*. What they perceive normally, they say to us correctly. Since we cannot perceive the way they perceive, for us, they are miracles. We, therefore, need to learn how to develop this kind of mind, also known as Intuitive Mind. We should not forget that when Carl Jung was struggling through his research in Switzerland to find out the universal level of the unconscious mind, Edgar Cayce at that time was devoting his life in America to giving the universal mind a voice. And by going into his trance state, he was successful in using the super-conscious mind and speaking to us what he was seeing.

CHARACTERISTICS OF THE SUPER-CONSCIOUS MIND

- It is the universal mind.
- It is like a mega computer connected to all the minds.
- It is connected to the Souls, Angels, and God.
- It is the all-knowing mind.
- It can transcend the bondage of time, space, and person and 'see' into the past, present, and future.
- It has the intuitive power and creative insight.
- It has many divine attributes like mercy, cheerfulness, spiritual ecstasy, humility, and enlightenment.
- It is an inexpressible joy.
- This level of mind can be achieved only through prayer and

regular practice of *yoga*.

- It has love, peace, and harmony for everyone.

HOW TO REACH THE SUPER-CONSCIOUS MIND

For reaching the Super-Conscious Mind, we need first to develop calm and quiet mind. This exercise suggested by Alan Seale may be of great help in reaching the point of stillness and connecting with the Spirit:

> "Sit quietly with your eyes closed, back straight, feet flat on the floor or legs folded in a lotus position, and hands resting comfortably on your lap. Take a few deep breaths, allowing your body to relax, and then let your breath find its own natural, relaxed, easy rhythm. Begin paying attention to your breath as it passes your nostrils. Bring all of your attention to that point of focus – breath passing through your nostrils. There is nothing else in your conscious awareness except the breath. ... As you are floating deeper, you may notice that you begin to feel calmer, more centred, and more grounded. You may feel your heart open. You are simply opening to you – your essence. You may become cognizant of several layers of awareness and consciousness at once. You may begin to understand on a whole new level of the meaning of "still waters run deep" – that on the surface there is lots of chatter, but the deeper you go the quieter it gets. Take your time to float for a while, and then when you feel as though the meditation is complete for now, open your eyes."

Today, in twenty-first century, more and more people are awaking to a call from within to open to the boundless possibilities of the greater world that seems hidden to normal conscious awareness. Therefore, Seale says further that to develop the ability to hear the voice of Spirit, one should follow the following five steps:

1. *Spiritual awakening*: An opening in conscious awareness to

the existence of Universal Force that is the creator and sustainer of all;

2. *Self-exploration*: Embarking upon a journey to uncover and know the divine essence of your being;
3. *Removing blocks*: Recognizing, acknowledging, and working through emotional blocks and inner resistance of fears that hinder a full awareness of your own divinity, and the constant flow of Love through you;
4. *Intuitive development*: Developing the intuitive mind as an aspect of Spirit, of Love, of God, of the Great Mystery;
5. *Surrender*: Complete surrender to the guidance of Spirit. This surrender is not at all a passive process. It is an active process of being in a profoundly heightened state of awareness, receiving the guidance of Spirit, and responding in the appropriate way through attitude and action.

AN INWARD JOURNEY: THE JOURNEY WITH SOUL

All mankind receives an inner call at one stage or the other to begin an inward journey. This journey is to find out our Heavenly Father and our divine state of consciousness. The journey consists of actual experiences and not the written accounts given in our religious books. They are simply a road map. It has been rightly said by an American poet, Walter Whitman, "Not I, not anyone can travel that road for you. You must travel it for yourself. It is not far, it is within reach. Perhaps you have been on it since you were born, and did not know. Perhaps it is everywhere on water and on land."

We should not forget that our whole existence is the result of a journey. This begins with the formation of a physical body in the womb caused by a journey of the male and female seeds and cells. Then, after birth, the same journey continues as biological, geographical, and psychological growth from one stage to another. Whether the organism is a human being or animal, it is born and should mature to its full potential, as an infant grows to an adult or a caterpillar develops into a butterfly. Although many try to develop their full potential, they get "stuck" in their mental and psychological growth due to poverty, socialization process, and other limitations. Even those who are fortunate, they have not gone beyond their good jobs and high salary. They have simply forgotten that it is the spiritual journey – the last developmental process – which completes the human's psyche. They have not only forgotten but also denied the spiritual component of mankind due to materialistic philosophy and scientific culture which does not believe in something which cannot be measured or observed. This has been a great mistake on their part. The spiritual journey makes them to realize that there is another existence and state beyond the physical. Today, even the quantum physics has started saying that "there is something", whether one wants to call it Spirit or not, that interacts with matter and energy and causes it to exist. Therefore, everyone needs to believe in spiritual journey and follow a transformational path to achieve love, peace, and harmony in their life. If they have the patience to continue on this path, they can be even free from the cycles of birth and death. Though there is not a fixed path which can be recommended for everyone, however, one can start with the teachings of Patanjali's *yoga* for living fully – physically and spiritually – without knowing the destination. It is bound to take him or her to a greater height and give some spiritual gifts without any side effect.

ENLIGHTENED LIVING: GETTING GUIDANCE FROM THE SOUL

Enlightenment is a goal that may be achieved through an inward journey. It begins with shifts in consciousness that release the mind, emotions, and body from conditioned concepts and cherished beliefs. The more we become self-aware and are able to open to Soul for guidance, the more the details of our lives seem to fall into place. Our personal responsibility in this process is first to remove any obstacles that might keep us away from hearing and seeing clearly what is being given to us, to listen and receive guidance, and then respond in the appropriate way and time. Thus, to "enlighten" is to provide spiritual insights into the true nature of life, to illuminate the divine, and to expand the human consciousness into the blissful freedom of complete enlightenment. To enter the enlightened consciousness is to leave behind all ignorant and erroneous perceptions that result in separation, greed, and hatred, and to live with only unity, love, compassion, and cooperation.

Since our Soul uses our brains, minds, and feelings and emotions to communicate with us, we get a lot of ideas, thoughts, images, and sounds in the beginning. We should allow them to flow spontaneously, and shculd not hold them back to "think" and experience about them. This will break the "connection" and flow of the information. The goal is to reach a point of allowing a constant stream of information through our conscious awareness so that we can receive guidance and proceed further accordingly. This may be a challenging task first, because we find ourselves wanting to "think" about what we are experiencing. But, gradually, we shall find that all such thoughts and images are being filtered by some mechanism, and only a few images keep coming up. We need to analyse and understand those images and work for them in future.

As children, we viewed the world with open, imaginative, and curious eyes. But today, as adults, we walk around with blinders on, only seeing the world from a limited point of view. The reason is: we see and interpret the world through our glasses of "Perceived Reality" which is different for different persons. There is nothing like one reality – it is just our "perceived reality" of it. For example, everybody knows that the sun rises in the east and sets in the west everyday. But, for a student of science, it is because the earth is moving round the sun, whereas, for an uneducated person, the sun is moving from east to west. Similarly, with rational mind, nobody can prove the existence of God. But, with intuitive mind, anybody can say that God exists. Thus, we need to realize that apart from physical realities, there are certain metaphysical realities which also influence and govern our lives. We, therefore, need to know about them, and get guidance from them for leading a happy and successful life. Though these realities are many, we need to know at least the following four, as suggested by Kelly Canull, for enlightened living:

- Each of us has a soul.
- Each of us has a unique purpose for being on earth which is encoded upon our soul.
- Everyday, we have an opportunity to ask our soul for clarity, guidance, and direction.
- Our soul will always show us an answer to our prayers, requests, questions, or inquiries.

The changes brought about by enlightened living are not merely adjustments to the *status quo*. They are innovative creations and ideas that completely eliminate the structures and concepts formed by materialistic consciousness. The outcome is unified and loving people start living together and enjoying without finding faults with anyone. There had been such persons in the past, though small in number, who liberated themselves mentally, emotionally, spiritually, and physically. But most of them lived in forests, remote mountains, and rural areas—far from crowded places. But today's thinking is that one can live the enlightened life "in the world", and there is no need to go far off in isolation. Secondly, there is no need to kill the ego and neglect the body to attain enlightenment as the *yogis* and sages were doing earlier. We simply need to maintain a balance among the three entities – body, mind, and spirit – with the help of ego. It is the ego, the physical body and personality that works as a powerful partner with the soul and provides vehicle through which our soul lives in the physical world. Soul and ego, therefore, need to work together as powerful partners to lead an enlightened life.

It has been rightly said by Canull, "We are at a critical time in history where the old foundation of fear is crumbling and we need to collectively create a new foundation of living as our Whole Self, founded in Divine Love. In order to do this, we must invite our dialoguing mind into silence". She suggests that by following a daily routine with the following seven exercises anybody can continue to move inward to the Truth of "Who We Really Are" and "How We Can Start Enlightened Living" without going anywhere else. However, before going on these exercises, she says that we should **create an altar** (a sacred space where we can sit and go inward for peace and tranquillity every morning) and **reawaken our divine essence** (to remember that we have divine power within us) so that we can do the following simple exercises very effectively:

1. **Set Your Intention for the Day:** Intention is something that we are consciously choosing to focus our attention on. It is a declaration of what we want to do today.
2. **Focus Your Thoughts through Candle Gazing:** Candle gazing is a wonderful way to become more aware of our thoughts. As we continue to use this tool day after day, our power of concentration goes up and up.
3. **Alignment Prayer:** By sending out our prayers daily, we are sending out our requests to the universe and are becoming conscious co creators of our world. The intention of this prayer is to align our lower self with the Higher Self.
4. **"I AM" Affirmations:** This is our intention about where we want our thoughts to go. Accordingly, we affirm and feel that we have got it.
5. **Gratitude:** When we express gratitude, we are giving love back to the Universe, establishing a flow of energy between our Self and the source of all things.
6. **Call in the Source of Your Inner Strength:** All we need is a pure intention to ask the Source of our inner strength to come into our life and guide us every day.
7. **Communicating with the Voice of Your Soul:** When we pray to God, actually, we are communicating with God; and when we meditate, actually, we are listening to God. Thus, it is a two-way communication with the higher self.

PURPOSE OF THIS BOOK

This book is about what the Super-Conscious Mind is and how it is connected with all other minds. It is beyond time and space and has the infinite intelligence to take all correct decisions. Since it is illuminated by the soul, it has got all the divine power of the soul to guide anyone of us on the spiritual path. We simply need to know how to get its guidance in self-discovery, inward journey, and enlightened living. This book, therefore, has been designed and structured in such a way that it can be a guidebook for a person to move on spiritual journey. There are only nine articles in this book, but each one is like a milestone on the way of journey where one may like to stop for a short while, take rest, and move further for the next milestone. At the end of covering all the milestones, one may feel relaxed, settled, and enlightened. Everyone will say that he or she has got something in the name of spiritual gifts while travelling on this path – it could be love, peace, and harmony or it could be something else like creative talents and career success. Thus, for everyone, this book has something to offer without any side effect. Some persons also may say that they have got answers for many of the puzzling questions by going through this book. For example, how some people in the past were successful in liberating themselves physically, mentally, emotionally, and spiritually by increasing their spiritual consciousness, and how some could even free themselves from the cycles of birth and death. Thus, this book will help everyone in knowing about the ultimate purpose of human life and "grand" design of God for creating the Universe.

It is a fact that anyone who has travelled on the path of spiritual journey has experienced a lot of difficulties on the way. But, at the end, each one has enjoyed and felt enlightened. It is, therefore, worth travelling and collecting spiritual gifts as much as one can. Perhaps, there is no other way or easy way to get the spiritual gifts.

M.B. SHARAN, Ph.D.
Senior Professor of Psychology
School of Humanities & Social Sciences
Indian Institute of Technology Patna, Bihar, India
E-mail: mbsharan@iitp.ac.in/mithilasharan@yahoo.co.in

1

Understanding of Human Mind and Behaviour: The Missing Link of Intuitive Experience

PSYCHOLOGY: GAINING CONSCIOUSNESS

Psychology began as the study of consciousness, and then turned to the study of observable behaviour. Today, it is the science of both: behaviour and mental processes. Thus, what psychology lost once (consciousness), it is gaining again with renewed vigour in the name of mental processes (Myers, 1986). Now, the question is: Why these swings of interest? Actually, in the beginning, the difficulty of studying consciousness scientifically led many psychologists to turn to direct observations of behaviour. But, by 1960, advances in neuroscience made it possible to relate brain activity to various mental states – waking, sleeping, and dreaming. As a result, today, many psychologists are affirming the importance of mental processes and are looking afresh into the power of infinite mind.

HUMAN MIND: CONSCIOUS, SUBCONSCIOUS OR UNCONSCIOUS ?

The nature of human mind, however, is very difficult to understand because it is very subtle as well as hidden. Therefore, it has been defined in different ways by different thinkers. Since Freud originally defined the structure of personality in terms of the unconscious, preconscious, and conscious, we psychologists have also been talking about the same topographical model all these years — 'conscious' as the part of the psyche that includes material of which one is fully aware; 'preconscious' (or 'subconscious') as the part of the psyche that includes material which is not at the moment within one's awareness, but which can readily be brought to the conscious mind; and 'unconscious' as the part of the psyche that includes material not within one's awareness and which cannot readily be brought to the conscious mind (Ewen, 1980). And thus, under the influence of Freud and his psychoanalysis, we have been recognizing unconscious factors as significant determinants of human behaviour.

Recently, however, a new debate between the "minds" has started and many of the thinkers and researchers are recommending to maintain a balance between the unconscious mind and the conscious/ subconscious mind. They are just a way of describing events— 'conscious' as whatever we are aware of at a moment, and 'unconscious' as everything else – that are useful in the context of therapeutic change (Bandler & Grinder, 1979). Otherwise, as a whole, we have only one mind. This can be supported by an example. Suppose, we are driving along the highway returning home; on approaching the neighbourhood, we start realizing that for the past several minutes our mind has been elsewhere. Daydreaming, thinking about things, our mind has been on anything but paying attention to the road. We wonder how we managed to watch out for cars, follow traffic signals, and make the right turns when we were "not there". Thus, there are a number of things we are doing without paying proper attention to all at a time and the pendulum of awareness swings between the "minds" without any difficulty.

Now, the question is: By which name should this one mind be known? Those who are working in the field of information processing say that conscious awareness is just the tip of the iceberg. It simply enables us to exert voluntary control and to communicate our mental states to others (Kihlstrom, 1987). Beneath the surface, actually, subconscious information processing occurs simultaneously on many parallel tracks. When we look at a flying bird, we are consciously aware of the result of our cognitive processing but not of our sub-processing of the bird's colour, form, movement, distance and identity. Therefore, from the functional viewpoint, it is the subconscious mind (including unconscious) which takes care of all the processes that are occurring out of conscious awareness. This one mind thus should be known as the subconscious mind.

Philosophers and some other thinkers, however, attach maximum importance to the conscious part of the mind. They say that it is the conscious part of the mind which does all the processing of information because it is logical, reasonable and can change its point of view at will. Since the subconscious mind is not logical and reasonable, it cannot take any independent decision of its own and it has to simply support the conscious mind. According to *Vedanta* (Ellis, 1994), the mind is called *antahkarana,* that is, internal instrument which perceives through five sense organs – eyes, ears, nose, tongue, and skin. It also instructs the five organs of action – the organ of speech, the hands, the legs, the organ of procreation, and the organ of evacuation. Thus, *Vedanta* recognizes the different functions of the mind – cognition, feeling and willing as the primary functions and memory, imagination, love, hatred, hope, fear, anger, etc., as the other functions. All these functions are possible only through the power of consciousness. And thus, the 'one mind' should be known as the conscious mind because it has the power to be illuminated by consciousness.

Vedanta says further that the power of consciousness, however, is not the built-in characteristic of the mind. This comes from some higher source known as *Soul, Atman* or *Self*. Since mind is not the real perceiver or knower of the mental phenomenon, Hindu religion differentiates between the mind and the Self – the mind as an object (the known) and the Self as a subject (the knower). Anything that falls into the category of the known does not have consciousness as its very essence whereas the subject or knower does. Thus, there is one ultimate observer or experiencer, and that is the Self. This is the reason why today many are also supporting the idea that there are three distinct factors of human personality – the physical body, the mind, and the soul. They are vitally connected and though they appear to be one single entity, they are distinguishable.

Recently, some Western psychologists (Reed, 1989) have also started talking about the "super-conscious" and the "universal" parts of the mind which were accepted by Indian thinkers ages ago. Since Freud did not support Jung's collective unconscious, the transpersonal mind remained neglected all these years. Otherwise, Jung was of the firm opinion that the unconscious mind gave us all the encouragement and help that a bountiful nature could shower on man. "It holds possibilities which are locked away from the conscious mind, for it has at its disposal all subliminal psychic contents, all those things which have been forgotten or overlooked, as well as the wisdom and experience of uncounted centuries which are laid down in its archetypal organs….The unconscious can serve man as a unique guide, provided he can resist the lure of being misguided" (Ellis, 1994). Thus, the unconscious mind should not be treated as the 'forgotten' mind or the dark side of the mind. It has many spiritual and moral possibilities hidden within it.

CONCLUSION: SUPER-CONSCIOUS MIND AS THE SOUL'S MIND

Now, the question is: What should we conclude from all these? We should not get caught by the words 'conscious', 'subconscious' and 'unconscious'. They are just to describe different functions of the same mind. There are conscious and considered thought, subconscious having recallable memories, habits, and old feelings, and unconscious having forgotten instincts, conditioning and collective or universal experiences. Each of these is accessible to us in some way because they communicate with each other in their own way. We should, therefore, try to develop such a mind which can perceive and judge things rightly making use of all the informations–

conscious, subconscious or unconscious. According to *Vedanta*, "The richest soil, the soil of the human mind, lies fallow. If it could be tilled well it would yield golden crops, but since it lies fallow, it yields brambles and thorny bushes and weeds" (Ellis, 1994). That means, if there are wrong tendencies lying within, they have to be weakened by constant effort. Since the subconscious and the unconscious mind work mechanically, such change is possible only by the conscious mind through its special power of self-determination. Thus, for the development of the mind, we have to feed the mind with rich food, nourish it regularly, strengthen it, and enrich it. As a result, we can have good understanding, peace, wisdom and joy. In this sense, our mind, illuminated by the Self, becomes the *Super-Conscious* or *Universal Mind*.

Super-Conscious Mind is thus the soul's mind which is connected to all others' minds. Edgar Cayce has given a pictorial model of the link between minds (Reed, 1989). It shows that there is one mind and people share it (see Figure 1.1).

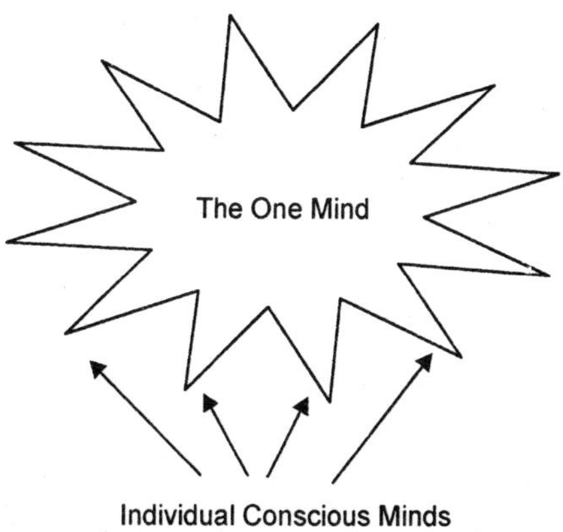

Fig. 1.1: The Relations between Individual Conscious Minds and the One Mind

In Figure 1.1, which is a multipoint star, Cayce shows how the star itself represents the entire mind. Each arm of the star represents a portion of the mind for a different person. The very tip of each point represents the conscious mind of an individual.

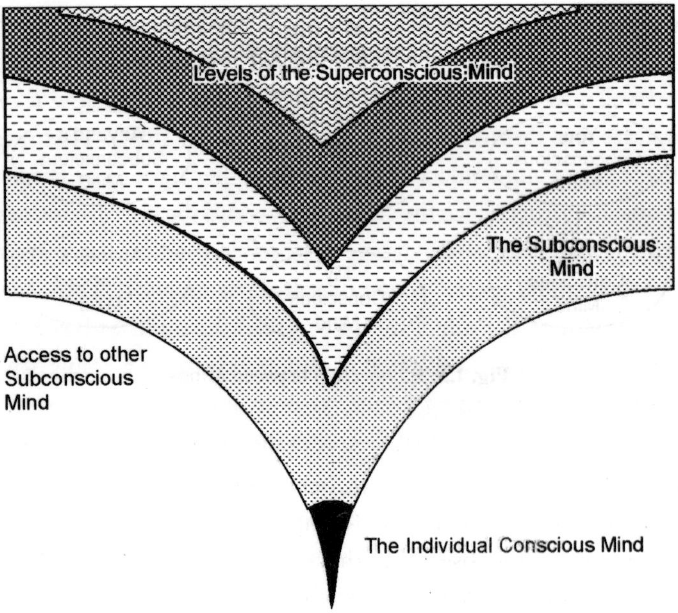

Fig. 1.2 : Regions of the Mind

In Figure 1.2, we see how the unconscious mind is a continuous connective layer of the inner parts of the mind's arms. The star tips only seem separate from one another. The arms of the stars are clearly like fingers on the same hand. The arms represent our subconscious minds. All subconscious minds are connected. The core of the mind is available to us all *via* the Super-Conscious Mind. The relationship between the conscious, subconscious, and Super-Conscious Mind is thus something like this (see Figure 1.3) as suggested by Koh (2004):

From the diagram, we can see that we are all connected at the super-conscious level, through our individual's subconscious mind.

HUMAN BEHAVIOUR: PHYSICAL, MENTAL OR SPIRITUAL?

American psychologists defined psychology as "the science of

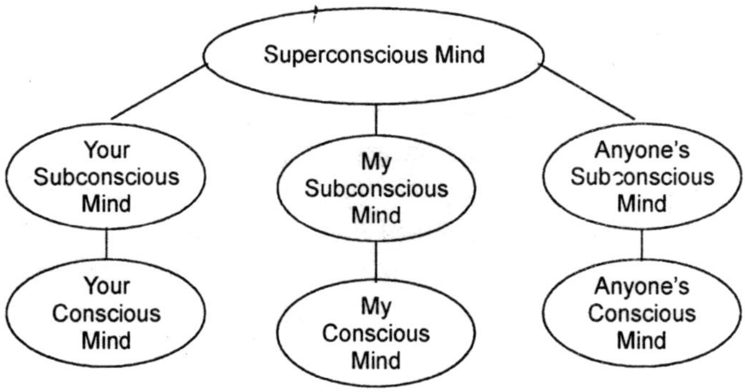

Fig. 1.3: Connection between Minds

observable behaviour". For them, behaviour was an overt activity of the organism. Since sensation, feeling and emotion (or anything subjective) were not observable, they could not be the subject matters of Psychology. As a result, many of the studies in Psychology remained restricted to overt activities of an organism for many-many years in the hands of behaviourists. But, today, we are not agreeing with the behaviourists and are studying mental processes in Psychology as well. Not only that, we also try to explain the human behaviour in terms of 'mind' involved in it. Since mind instructs the body to behave in a definite way, the resultant behaviour is having minimum two aspects – *the physical,* and *the mental.* In order to have an effective behaviour, we try to maintain a balance between the two. In this process, the effective behaviour, in which mind and body work together without dominating upon each other, becomes "spiritual" in nature due to Gestalt effect. We can take the example of understanding love in a laboratory. Is it not a fact that by putting love under scientific scrutiny, we are destroying its mystery? In reality, love includes affection and anger, excitement and boredom, stability and change, bond and freedom, etc. This, therefore, cannot be known by any scientific method. As a result, those researchers, who have tried to know about it by using all sorts of sophisticated instruments, have found it to be a 'triangle' having three sides: physiological, psychological, and anthropological. But, outside the laboratory, the "true love" has emerged as a 'circle' which combines all the three sides into one. This organization as a whole is known as "spiritual love" in which all the parts are merged with each other. This is such a nice blend that no factor is dominating upon anyone. This kind of "true love" cannot be analyzed but can be experienced. Like this, every human behaviour needs to be effective (spiritual) and needs to be understood finally by experience. And such experience is known as "Intuitive Experience."

CAN INTUITION BE ONE OF THE METHODS OF PSYCHOLOGY?

In any science, the methods of investigation depend largely on the subject matter. Accordingly, like all scientists, psychologists construct theories that organize observations and imply testable hypotheses. To describe, predict, and explain behaviour and mental processes, psychologists use several methods: Introspection, Naturalistic Observation, Questionnaire and Survey, Case Study, Correlation and Experimentation. Every method has been found to be useful but, at the same time, suffering from certain limitations. Even the experimental method, which is considered to be the ultimate method of Psychology today, is subject to certain serious objections. "For many thoughtful students the idea of applying science to human affairs raises concerns about how well experiments relate to life, how experimenters treat human and animal subjects, and how psychologists' values influence their work and its applications" (Myers, 1986). In such situation, as suggested by a good number of Indian thinkers and Western scientists (e.g., McDermott, 1970; Fitz, 2001; Denning, 2001), Intuition can be a very useful, and perhaps the only method in some cases, in Psychology. We all have this system in place but, the irony is, we have not yet learned how to use it fully; we just need to recognize it, to tune in to our intuition (Clare, 2003). According to Denning (2001), "Everyone has intuition; we could not live without it. It is just more highly developed in some people than in others. Most people are unaware of their intuitive abilities and, therefore, do not use them to their advantage". Even Einstein, one of the towering intellects of modern time, remarked once, "The intuitive mind is a sacred gift and the rational mind is a faithful servant. We have created a society that honours the servant and has forgotten the gift".

WHAT IS INTUITION?

The term "intuition" means exactly what it sounds like in-tuition – an inner tutor or teaching and learning mechanism that takes us forward daily. The dictionary defines intuition as "the perception of truths, facts, etc., without reasoning; the immediate knowledge or learning of something without the conscious use of reasoning; instantaneous apprehension". That means, it is a process which perceives things without relying on the senses and gives us a kind of creative awareness by interpreting all the informations in a holistic way. Keeping all these in mind, Swami Omkarananda (1999) has rightly said, "Intuition is the immediate knowledge of the Absolute, obtained through the eye of wisdom, as opposed to the knowledge of the external objects derived through the exercise of the senses and the intellect. It is truth obtained by internal apprehension, without the aid of perception or the operation of the reasoning powers. It is a direct vision and apprehension of the Divine Reality underlying the manifested and the unmanifested universe".

Day (1996), while defining intuition as a nonlinear and nonempirical process of gaining and interpreting information, says further that intuition responds to questions. All our senses – touch, sight, smell, hearing and taste – respond to the questions our environment and our "body machine" pose. Our rational mind interprets the information provided by these senses for more efficient survival. And intuition's function is to bring to consciousness that information which lies beyond what our rational mind perceives from our five senses: people we don't know, places we have not been to or the future.

HOW CAN WE HAVE THE INTUITIVE EXPERIENCE?

Many belief systems teach that staying present or being 'mindful' is the basic principle behind inner peace and contentment which leads to intuitive experience. Being mindful means giving full concentration to whatever we are doing in the present, having no real awareness of anything else, becoming completely absorbed, lost in the activity and the moment. According to Clare (2003), "this experience of the moment means we are far more likely to notice things around us....". This suggests that intuition comes to a person only when he or she has the intuitive state of mind. It involves more than simply "going with our gut" or "trusting our hunches". It is also not synchronicity. It prompts a person to think in certain ways that create the results which contribute to well-being, allowing synchronicity to manifest (Denning, 2001). According to Reed and English (2000), by paying attention to the thoughts, feelings, and images that come to mind, we are learning to tune into our intuition which is a natural gift born in everyone. But it becomes most effective in a person who learns to develop *The Intuitive Heart* by caring and loving his/her own inner self and of others. In order to have the intuitive experience through The Intuitive Heart, Reed and English suggest the following six steps:

- **Learn from Your Breath to Trust Your Intuitive Inspiration:** Focus on your breathing and discover how you can trust it to flow naturally, spontaneously, with no effort or control on your part. Intuitive inspiration will come to you automatically.
- **Make the Heart Connection:** Let gratitude fill your heart, allowing you to release all concerns. Your heart energy naturally begins to expand. Focus it on the target of your search for intuition.
- **Invite a Memory**: Ask for one of your millions of personal memories to pop into your mind. Without intentionally choosing it, but accepting the first one that comes, trust

that within your heart is stored the perfect memory that is just right for this occasion.

- **Tell Your Story:** Explore the experience that surrounds that memory. Let your memory be the seed of a story – here's what was going on, here's what happened, here's how it turned out.
- **Search Your Heart for Wisdom:** See what lessons your story holds. What truths does it contain? What did you learn from that experience? What does this story teach you today?
- **Learn from Feedback:** Note how the teaching story relates to the focus of your quest for intuition. How can you use this new perspective to respond to your current situation differently?

INTUITION AS THE ONLY METHOD OF KNOWING TRUTH

Modern science, particularly Psychology which wants to understand today the Super-Conscious mind and spiritual behaviour of human beings, must come to realize that, ultimately, the method of intuition is the only method of discerning the truth. Without developing the intuition, the intellectual remains imperfect and blind to the truth behind the appearances. According to Swami Omkarananda (1999), "Intuition is the only way by which the Absolute can be realized and experienced in all its totality. The mortal, finite, limited senses and the intellect, cannot comprehend the Reality which is immortal and all-pervading". This is the reason why all *Courses in Miracles* are teaching today to have regular prayer (talking to God) and meditation (listening to God) to have His grace for developing Intuitive Mind.

REFERENCES

Bandler, R.; & Grinder, J. (1979). *Frogs into Princes: Neuro-Linguistic Programming.* UT: Real People Press.

Clare, S. (2003). *Trust Your Intuition* (2nd ed.). Delhi: Macmillan.

Day, L. (1996). *Practical Intuition.* New York: Broadway Books.

Denning, H. M. (2001). *Intuition and Synchronicity.* Virginia: A.R.E. Press.

Ellis, R. (Ed.). (1994). *Mind: According to Vedanta.* Madras: Sri Ramkrishna Math.

Ewen, R. B. (1980). *An Introduction to Theories of Personality.* New York: Academic Press.

Fitz, H. K. (2001). *Intuition: Its Nature and Uses in Human Experience.* Delhi: Motilal Banarsidas.

Kihlstrom, J. F. (1987). The cognitive unconscious. *Science, 237,* 1445-1452.

Koh, K. (2004). Mind power explained. www.subconscioussecrets.com

McDermott, R. A. (Ed.). (1970). *Basic Writings of S. Radhakrishnan.* Bombay; Jaico Publishing house.

Myers, D. G. (1986). *Psychology* (4th ed.). New York: Worth Publishers.

Reed, H. (1989). *Edgar Cayce on Mysteries of the Mind.* New York: Warner Books.

Reed, H. & English, B. (2002). *The Intuitive Heart.* Virginia: A.R.E. Press.

Swami, Omkarananda. (1999). *The Intuitive Experience of the Truth* (WWW ed.). Switzerland: DLZ-Service.

2

Spiritual Development and Counselling for College Students*

WHAT IS SPIRITUALITY?

Spirituality is a new buzz-word. It is being used today quite frequently with different meanings. Traditionally, being spiritual signified having an attachment to religious values, or matters related to spirit, rather than material or worldly interests. Recently, it has also taken as to mean reaching higher levels of consciousness using yoga, prayer, meditation and similar other practices. Therefore, it has been rightly said that it is a state of mind in which we are connected to God, Nature, each other, and the deepest part of ourselves.

A human being is a combination of three entities: body, mind and spirit. In order to function fully, we need to be in harmony with each other and maintain a balance among these three. Is it not a fact that we become spiritual when we enjoy listening to a beautiful piece of music, looking at an amazing work of art, or reading an inspirational poem? We become spiritual because when we are immersed in, it touches our soul and connects us to the artist and the creation itself (God). We experience a spiritual connection with

* This article was co-authored by Premshila Sharan, Senior Lecturer in Psychology, Madan Ahilya Women's College, Naugachhia, Bhagalpur, Bihar.

others when we work together to reach a common goal, such as raising a fund to help those in need, being in a musical band or orchestra, or anything that involves mutual love and cooperation. Thus, when we are in tune with God, Nature, or His any other creation, we become spiritual. There are so many wonderful ways that we can make, and take time to "connect" with spirit or God. For example:

1. By taking time for ourselves: By listening to relaxing music; reading some inspirational writings, etc.
2. By helping those in need of our assistance: When we help others, we automatically get a different kind of feeling of satisfaction.
3. By practising gratitude: There are so many things for which we can be grateful to God, our family members, and friends.
4. By practising mindfulness: When we sit for prayer or meditation, we feel automatically connected to some higher power.
5. By expressing ourselves: Every person has some creative talents which attract others. It could be playing a musical instrument, singing or dancing and getting lost in it.

Being aware of and cultivating spirituality greatly contributes to our overall joy and happiness (enlightenment). It is never too late to develop it further and enjoy the benefits it brings.

SPIRITUAL DEVELOPMENT

The word "spirituality" has a root that is spirit. This suggests some reference to the unseen. So by implication, it should be confined to that eternal part of humanity — the soul or *atman* that does not die. This is the reason why Clark describes it as the inner experience of the individual when he/she senses a Beyond. This Beyond could be soul, gods, supernatural power, or ancestors. Therefore, some persons define spirituality in terms of developing relationships with these eternals. In a nutshell, spirituality deals with issues of inner beliefs and feelings. This is the beauty of spiritual development; tapping into the part of mind and soul that is so deep and so driven that it can change our thinking, health and life. So in one word, spiritual development depends on faith.

The stages of spiritual development begin with a start-up seed. We need to see that it gets all it needs to grow and be a part of our everyday life. It is said that a healthy mind is in a healthy body, and a healthy soul is in a healthy mind. Therefore, spiritual development is for development of all the entities: body, mind and spirit. Once we start this inward journey, we realize that our Soul is a God given gift — our unseen navigation system, and there are many ways in which we can attune to this system. Edgar Cayce readings suggest the following seven ways:

1. **Prayer:** It is talking to God.
2. **Meditation:** It is listening to God.
3. **Study of Dreams:** Dreams reveal all the spiritual and moral possibilities hidden within the unconscious mind.
4. **Service to Others:** Service to others is the greatest service to God.
5. **Purpose of Life:** The quest for understanding the deeper meaning of life is the turning point in the life of individuals.
6. **Establishment of Ideals:** Ideal is the principle behind what we think, say and do—the patterns that we use to measure and shape our life.
7. **Law of Guidance:** There are three laws that define how to get the guidance we need in order to deal with any situation in our lives: (a) Seek first the spirit within, and you will find, (b) Ask the spirit with faith, and you will receive, and (c) Knock, with faith in spirit, and the door will be opened.

WHAT IS SPIRITUAL COUNSELLING?

We have seen that spiritual development depends primarily on Faith:

Faith in Self, Faith in potential, Faith in inward journey, and Faith in Spirit and/or God. It is something that can help us in times of trouble, stress, fear, and uncertainty. This is the reason why spiritual counselling has become important today for everyone. Spiritual counselling thus has an extended view of life: it takes into account belief systems, universal and personal energy systems, intuitive psychic realities, *karmic* interplay, subconscious and super-conscious states of awareness, and higher-self cosmic connections.

WHAT IS COUNSELLING FOR COLLEGE STUDENTS?

The term "counselling" is used generally for giving an expert advice to others. But in educational institutions, it is primarily a way of addressing and resolving problems related to students. It is an interactive process characterized by a unique relationship between counsellor and client that leads to change in the client. The counsellor acts as a facilitator in helping clients to understand feelings, behaviours, relationships with others, situations, choices and decisions.

PERSONAL AND PSYCHOLOGICAL PROBLEMS OF COLLEGE STUDENTS

College and university students must adapt to environments plagued by rapid change, ambiguity, uncertainty, and depleted support systems. They must also cope with a myriad of personal and psychological problems that range from basic adjustment, poor academic performance, and career concerns to clinical-level mental illness. Therefore, a comprehensive view of counselling is needed in the institutions of higher learning — not only educational, career, and developmental services. The aim of this kind of counselling is to help clients express themselves and their world with intimate wisdom, spiritual awareness and personal authenticity — using integrity and wise use of their spiritual gifts, skills, and knowledge.

Recently, there has been a big concern for looking into the cases of failures and suicides in institutes like IITs and IIMs. It has surprised many how students coming through the toughest exams like the J.E.E., MAT or CAT are failing in some subjects and committing suicides. Some are even not attending their classes properly and are abusing Internet services just for fun and erotic pleasure. Researches suggest that these students are doing badly in the examinations not because they lack intellectual abilities but they lack the following 'effective study skills':

1. They don't know how to listen to their teachers in the classroom.
2. They don't know how to concentrate and have confidence.
3. They don't know how to study and prepare notes.
4. They don't know how to face interviews and take tests and examinations.

Therefore, it has been rightly suggested that the counselling programme should extend its activities to take care of such study skills so that they develop good study habits.

HOW TO LISTEN?

Listening is different from hearing because body language of the speaker is also involved in it. It is an important element in any successful conversation. Most of the input that students receive comes from listening in class. Therefore, students who listen well have a marked advantage over students who do not listen. The main purpose of in-class listening is to understand and identify the information one will need later. Usually, our mind is filled with the daily activities of living. Therefore, to listen to someone, we need to pay extra attention. This is known as 'Active Listening' which suggests that:

1. Always 'listen' with your eyes as well as with your ears.
2. Look at the speaker directly.
3. Put aside distracting thoughts and environmental factors.
4. 'Listen' to the speaker's body language.
5. Recognize that listening has to be learnt and practised.

HOW TO CONCENTRATE AND HAVE CONFIDENCE?

Concentration is the ability to focus on a single object, idea, concept or problem, while remaining aware of what is going on around. It has powerful effects when it is used correctly as it is indispensable to becoming successful in all aspects of life. Studies show that the more one concentrates on something, the faster he/she attains them. To improve concentration, following steps are suggested:

1. *Relax*: As you prepare to concentrate, try to clear your mind of everything except the material you are working on. For this, you need to sit on a comfortable chair at a quiet place and start breathing slowly for about 5 minutes.
2. *Concentrate on one object for two minutes*: To start with, try to concentrate on one object for a few seconds. Then, go on increasing for two minutes. If any negative thought comes to your mind, just pull your mind back to the object.
3. *Concentrate on the same object for additional four minutes*: Your goal is to free your mind from all the thoughts and focus on the object of your choice for additional four minutes that you want to accomplish and attract into your life.
4. *Do this exercise a few times daily*: Learning how to concentrate and focus has many benefits such as peace of mind, improving your memory, controlling your thoughts, and becoming better at meditation and visualization. The more you practice the art of concentration, the faster you will master it.
5. *Set definite time period for how long you want to work*: Try to work

in short stretches, 20 minutes or so at a time with 10 minutes break at the end of each stretch.

6. Confidence is a belief and an assurance in one's own abilities or in the abilities of another person. In short, it is essentially a feeling secured of having an expected success. Improved concentration leads to better learning which ultimately leads to higher confidence.

HOW TO STUDY AND PREPARE NOTES?

Study is done to (a) develop a broad understanding of the study materials, and (b) identify the specific information to be learnt. The SQ3R method has been a proven way to sharpen study skills in which S stands for Survey, Q for Question, and 3R for Read, Recite and Review.

1. **Survey:** Get the best overall picture of what you are going to study. It is like looking at a road map before going on a trip.
2. **Question:** Ask questions for learning. Questions should include about headings, sub-headings, graphs, tables, etc., and emphasize on what, why, how, when, who, and where of the study contents.
3. **Read:** Reading is not running eyes over a textbook. Read actively to answer questions you have asked yourself.
4. **Recite:** After reading for about 20 to 30 minutes, one should try to recall what he/she has learnt.
5. **Review:** A review is a survey of what one has read. It is something like summarizing or counting main points on the fingers without seeing the book.

Even if a person is a good reader or a good listener, he/she is sure to forget the large majority of what he/she has learnt. Therefore, preparing notes is a must for all. Everyone should keep the following points in mind while preparing notes:

1. Having an accurate, reliable set of notes for each class is critical to effective study.
2. Note-taking is a skill which must be learned and refined.
3. Everyone should learn to keep notes legibly and logically.
4. The best place to keep notes is in a loose-leaf notebook.

HOW TO FACE INTERVIEWS AND TAKE TESTS AND EXAMINATIONS?

Interviews are the most common means of selecting employees. Therefore, everyone needs to master interview skills. One purpose of the interview is to allow the candidate to communicate with the interviewers using verbal and non-verbal communication skills. In addition, interviewers are also seeking to establish intellectual skills of a candidate to solve various problems of their organizations. Every candidate, therefore, needs to remember a number of points:

1. Always look at the interviewer and other members of the panel.
2. Use effective verbal and non-verbal communication skills.
3. Always be positive and optimistic when you are replying to questions.
4. Never be derogatory, cynical, facetious or sarcastic.
5. Be honest, don't invent answers.
6. Answer the question that is posed, not the one that you wish had been asked.
7. If you don't understand the question, ask for it to be repeated.

The major output measure in a school or a college is usually test or examination. Most of the time, students are graded primarily on the basis of correct answers. As one progresses in college, themes, essays, and papers become more important to their grades, but tests never disappear. Therefore, throughout the test, one should try to remain relaxed and should follow the following guidelines:

1. Begin to go through the test paper carefully as soon as it comes to your desk.
2. Before you begin answering, preview the test — what type of questions are there, how many of each type are included. Get a feel for the test as a whole.
3. At the end, make a point to check your answers before you submit your answer book.
4. Learn from the mistakes you committed in the past

A FINAL WORD

Before you even begin to learn about the process of learning, you should develop a schedule. If you don't have a schedule or a plan of study, then you will not have any way of allocating your valuable time when the unexpected comes up. A good, well thought out schedule can be a lifesaver. It is up to you to learn how to develop a schedule that meets your needs, revise it if necessary and most important, follow it. Thus, the success of study skills depends on your good study habits and on your Faith in self and Faith in Spirit or God.

REFERENCES

Hind, D.WG., and Moss, S. (2007). *Employability Skills.* Great Britain: Business Education Publishers.

Luckie, W.R., and Smethurst, W. (1998). *Study Power.* Massachusetts: Brookline Books.

Marques, J.; Dhiman, S.; and King, R. (2008). *Spirituality in the Workplace: What it is Why it Matters How to Make it Work for You.* Delhi: McMillan India.

3

Social Transformation through the Practice of Yoga

WHAT IS YOGA?

Yoga is one of the most ancient cultural heritages of India. It is a systematic way of establishing connections among body, mind, and spirit. In a traditional sense, it is a technique to unite individual *atma* (soul) with *Parmatma* (Universal Soul). In Sanskrit, the term "yoga" stands for "union". Therefore, the ultimate aim of yoga is to be able to attain this "union of the lower self to the higher Self" with the help of certain mental and physical exercises. It is a holistic way of living and healing, aimed at uniting the mind, body, and spirit. Today, it is an accepted practice throughout the world for improving physical fitness, mental clarity, self-understanding, and general well-being. It is an exercise in moral and mental cultivation that generates good health, contributes to longevity and the total intrinsic discipline culminates into positive and perennial happiness and peace. It is a science that affects not only the conscious self but the subconscious as well. It is a practical physiological training, which if practised properly, can exalt man to the "super-conscious level".

Developed in India about 5,000 years ego, it is an ancient psycho-physical discipline which teaches about how to unite with the Absolute. It is the result of human wisdom and insight on physiology, psychology, ethics, and spirituality collected together and practised over thousands of years for the well-being of humanity. Credit goes to the Indian sage, Patanjali who made it popular and systematic by writing *"The Yog-Sutra"* and summarizing the various aspects of yoga in the following eight limbs:

1. *Yama:* Restraint of Negative Behaviour.
2. *Niyama:* Observance of Positive Behaviour.
3. *Asana:* Yoga Postures.
4. *Pranayama:* Breathing and Energy.
5. *Pratyahara:* Sensory Mastery.
6. *Dharana:* Concentration.
7. *Dhyana:* Meditation.
8. *Samadhi:* Perfect Concentration.

Yoga is thus an all-embracing way of life, a science of self-culture and mental discipline which ensures the purgation of the ignoble in man and brings forth what is most noble in him. It is pertinent to all people irrespective of his caste, creed, sex and religion. It can be beneficial to all — the good and the bad, the sick and the healthy, the believer and the non-believer, the literate and the ignorant, the young and the old. A person may begin yoga at any age and can go on reaping its benefits.

BENEFITS OF YOGA

- **The physical benefits:** Creates a toned, flexible, and strong body. Improves respiration, energy, and vitality. Helps to maintain a balanced metabolism. Promotes cardio and circulatory health. Relieves pain. Helps one look and feel younger than of his age. Improves his athletic performance.
- **The mental benefits:** Helps one relax and handle stressful situations more easily. Teaches about how to quiet the mind so that one can focus his energy where he wants it to go — into a difficult yoga pose, on the tennis court or golf course,

or in the office. Encourages positive thoughts and self-acceptance.

- **The spiritual benefits:** Builds awareness of his body, his feelings about the world around, and the needs of others. Promotes interdependence between mind, body, and spirit. Brings about a profound spiritual and social transformation. Helps in living the concept of "oneness" and enjoying peace and happiness in life.

BALANCING THE THREE ENTITIES: BODY, MIND, AND SPIRIT

Balance in life is one of the simplest concepts of healthy living, but it is also one of the most difficult to find. There is so much that threatens to pull us to one extreme or another — it could be eating, investing time and energy, or relating to other people. Therefore, in order to have a healthy lifestyle, we need to maintain a balance among body, mind, and spirit.

A human being is a combination of body, mind, and spirit. The body is the physical residue of the soul's expression as the vibrational energy of the soul has been patterned by images created in the mind. Therefore, Edgar Cayce says rightly, "Spirit is the life, mind is the builder, and physical is the result." Creativity begins as pure energy, but changes by assuming a specific pattern. As a vibrational pattern, the energy contains information. The informational pattern has a way of working itself down from the very abstract, invisible level to the concrete, material level of reality. Thus, there is a continuous correspondence among body, mind, and spirit.

Body

Our physical body has three different types of systems: *Physical, Sensory, and Energy*. The physical body has eleven separate, yet interdependent, major physical systems. Many of these have sub-systems of their own. These systems are:

Digestive: This is the system that breaks down food and absorbs its nutrients. The digestive tract is a long system of tubes that run from the mouth to the anus. It includes the esophagus, stomach, small intestine, and large intestine. The liver and the pancreas manufacture special enzymes to help break down food.

Muscular: This system provides the body with movement. There are three types of muscle: skeletal, cardiac, and smooth. Skeletal muscles attach to bones, and are voluntary — they are consciously controlled by the nervous system. Cardiac muscles cause the heart to pump blood and are involuntary.

Integumentary: The integumentary system includes skin, which provides sensory receptors and protects the body.

Excretory: This system gets rid of various body wastes. It includes the sweat glands (where the body excretes unnecessary salts), kidneys (which filter the blood), and urinary tract.

Reproductive: The reproductive system allows for the continuation of life. Gametes from the male's sperm and the female's egg combine to form a zygote — a unique combination of genes which no other human being has.

Circulatory: This is the system that our blood flows through. It carries nutrients and oxygen to all the organs of the body, and carries away wastes.

Respiratory: The respiratory system provides the body with oxygen, and it expels carbon dioxide from the body. The nasal passage, trachea, bronchial tubes, lungs, and alveoli are involved in this process.

Skeletal: The skeletal system provides structure for the body and protection for the body's internal organs. Bones, ligaments, joints, and the skull are all parts of the skeleton.

Immune: The body's immune system fights disease. The lymphatic system is the main defense mechanism within this system. A liquid called lymph flows over the tissues and carries off harmful bacteria, which is filtered out in the lymph nodes.

Nervous: The brain, spinal cord, and nerves work together to coordinate the body's actions. Our senses are also part of this system, allowing us to see, taste, smell, touch, hear, and feel pressure and pain.

Endocrine: The endocrine system tells the body how to develop. It does that by releasing hormones that contain instructions to cells about how to grow. Hormones affect organs and glands by telling them how to operate. The nervous system and endocrine system usually work together.

Additionally, we have a sensory system that includes taste, touch, sight, feel, smell, equilibrium, and the less frequently talked about *clairs*. Clair is the French word for clear, and to some degree we all have clairvoyance or clear seeing; clairaudience or clear hearing; clairsentience or clear feeling; and Clair cognizance or clear knowing.

Similarly, we have energy system because our body is sustained by life force energy. The laws governing quantum physics demonstrate that everything in the universe is made up of vibrational fields — the human body is no exception. Located on the mid-line of the body there are seven major transition points for the distribution of life force energy. These are known as *chakras* (energy stations). There are seven *chakras* in all: Root (*Muladhara*), Sacral (*Svadhisthana*), Solar Plexus (*Manipura*), Heart (*Anahata*), Throat (*Vishuddha*), Third Eye (*Ajna*), and Crown (*Sahasrara*). Energy travels from these stations on distribution paths that are similar to a highway system. They are known as *meridians* (energy pathways). The energy that travels through the meridians feeds all of the organs, glands, body systems, and sub-systems — ultimately every muscle, nerve, tissue, and cell. Surrounding the outside of the body there are several electrical energy fields which are collectively referred to as the electromagnetic field; human energy field (HEF); or *aura* (energy shell).The *chakras*, meridians, and aura are intrinsically linked — forming an intricate network that distributes life force energy. It is this complex system of energy transfer and distribution that is the focus of all energy-based therapies.

Mind

According to *Vedanta*, the mind is known as *antahkarana* (internal instrument) which perceives through five sense organs — eyes, ears, nose, tongue, and skin - and acts through five organs of action — the organ of speech, the hands, the legs, the organ of procreation, and the organ of evacuation. Thus, it recognizes different functions of the mind and thereby assumes that all these functions are possible only through the conscious mind. The power of consciousness, however, *Vedanta* says further, is not the built-in characteristic of the mind. This comes from some higher source known as *Soul, Atman* or *Self.* Since mind is not the real perceiver or knower of the mental phenomenon, *Vedanta* differentiates between the mind and the Soul — the mind as an object (the known) and the Soul as a subject (the knower). Anything that falls into the category of the known does not have consciousness as its very essence whereas the subject or knower does. Thus, there is one ultimate observer or experiencer, and that is the Soul. This is the reason why today many are of the opinion that there are three distinct factors of human personality — the physical body, the mind, and the soul. They are vitally connected and though they appear to be one single entity, they are distinguishable. Thus, it can be safely concluded that one should not get caught by the words 'conscious', 'subconscious' and 'unconscious' parts of the mind because they are just to describe different functions of the same mind. Each of these is accessible to us in some way because they communicate with each other in their own way. This one mind, therefore, should be best known as the conscious mind.

Spirit

The spirit is the vital principal in humans — it is our very essence, our being, our soul. The spiritual part of humans is distinctly separate from the physical part. It is our inner self — the unseen part of us. It is divine. Unlike the body and mind which are interdependent, it is a different entity, separable from the body. It departs from our physical body upon death. The soul's responsibility, in part, is to guide the personality (thinking, feeling, and will) to determine and fulfil its life's purpose. Many metaphysicians believe that illnesses and diseases begin in the emotional, mental, and spiritual energies that are in and around us. Therefore, a regular practice of yoga is the only holistic way of life that unites to the body, mind, and spirit for complete health and well-being.

YOGA AS A TRANSFORMATIONAL PROCESS

While people practices yoga for many reasons, everyone comes to realize its benefits of self-improvement and healing. Self-improvement is at many levels including intention, attitude, posture, breathing, archetypes, energy centres, concentration, locks and seals, psychological blocks, and emotions. Thus, there is a complete change in the personality of a person through yoga. Such changes are at least at four levels: physical health, mental health, social health, and spiritual health.

But apart from these changes at individual level, there are also changes at environmental and societal levels. Like a temple, the flavour of yoga starts influencing the people and the environment around. Since the eight aspects of yoga comprise a subjective art, science, and philosophy which covers the five layers of the human being: the anatomical, physiological, mental, intellectual and spiritual bodies, they also balance the ecosystem and environment of the elements (earth, water, fire, air, ether). These ethical principles sustain friendliness, compassion, and happiness all around. Similarly, the five principles of *yama:* non-violence, truthfulness, non-misappropriation, chastity, and non-possessiveness introduce universal ethical culture to be followed by one and all, irrespective of race, gender, colour, or climate. And those who go against *yama* face imbalances, not only in their family but also within the society and community. These imbalances become the cause of death to the Self, even while the person remains alive.

We are made of our ancestry — earth, air, water, etc. But when we deny these origins due to our self-interests, we turn those elements into commodities rather than resources. We measure water in terms of its exportability, forests in terms of their cubic feet, and lands in terms of their real estate value. Through such unethical business practices, people have become "consumers" and commodities are categorized as "markets" or "sectors." At a psychological level, the self is also commercialized when it is treated as an object to be improved and perfected.

Thus, if we want to plant positive seeds in the mind and body, we need to do two things to change. First, we need to understand the causal relationship between our actions and the effects of our actions. Second, once sensitive to the devastating effect of our actions in the human and non-human world, we need practical skills for learning how to take action, especially when our minds are caught up in reactivity and distraction and are unable to touch the present moment. Yoga helps in doing both the things – understanding causal relationship between actions and effects and developing practical skills to remove the devastating effects by raising global consciousness.

HOW GLOBAL CONSCIOUSNESS IS RAISED THROUGH THE PRACTICE OF YOGA

Primarily, transformation is a personal inner process. It starts first at the individual level. Then, it goes on spreading. A happy person makes his family happy; a happy family makes a happy community and society; and finally, a happy society makes a happy nation. This way yoga contributes to peace and sustainability at global level. Therefore, Swami Vivekananda gave the formula: "Be and Make." Here, the 'be' is the first thing that we have to do. That means, everyone of us should start practising yoga first, and then should 'make' a determination of transforming ourselves from *Tamas* to *Rajas* and from *Rajas* to *Sattva*. And this transformation in all of us will lead to harmony, love, and peace in the society. This is something automatic based on the principle of quantum physics. In Quantum Physics it is very well known that if in a chamber there are molecules, normally they have the tendency to move here and there randomly. But by some process of magnetic induction when they are attracted to move, they start moving in that particular direction. Quantum Physics also shows how we are all connected, how we are all One Being. It explains how Spirit and Matter interact and connect; how Mind and Matter do so as well. This way, we are creating everything ourselves. Now, we can understand how collective faith and right thinking work together as a powerful force and attract the mass to have a similar faith and confidence. It has been rightly said that even if one per cent of the population starts doing yoga properly, then all the other persons start moving in the same direction. This does not mean that all others will also start doing yoga but they are affected by the thoughts of yoga of harmony, peace, and love. Thus, there is a complete change in the society automatically through this global consciousness.

Actually, our body is made up of cells. These cells are in turn made up of molecules, which are made up of atoms, which are in turn made up of sub-atomic particles such as electrons. But we should keep in mind that though the atomic and larger particles look like objects or things, but they are not objects as such. They are both wave-like and particle-like at the same time. This is the world of Quantum Physics where all that exists is ultimately energy, and the way in which energy manifests into recognizable form depends on its vibrational frequency. High frequencies are more effective transmitters than low frequencies, but they become less recognizable to the human senses. Matter can be seen as energy functioning at much lower frequencies. There is a level at which energy cannot exist in the material world, but it can exist in other dimensions of extremely high frequencies, as in another octave above the one we experience. This energy of Quantum Physics has a telepathic effect among atomic particles which express through their rotary action. It is there that the patterns of psychic energy and patterns of physical processes become 'One'. This 'One' in *Vedanta* is known as consciousness which is spread across time and space. The *Bhagavad Gita* also says that as the sun alone illuminates this universe, so does the living entity, one within the body, illuminates the entire body by consciousness.

This is the reason why good thoughts, beliefs, ideas, etc., generated by yoga start influencing the world around in a positive way. In this sense, we are co-creators with God because all — good and bad — has been created by us. We, therefore, have the power to create good things and eliminate bad things by creating magnetic force of good intention as taught by yoga. God is always with us in this kind of creation, if our intention is good.

REFERENCES

Butera, R. (2010). *The Pure Heart of Yoga.* Woodbury, MN: Llewellyn Publications.
Reed, H. (1968). *Awakening Your Psychic Powers.* New York: St. Martin's Paperbacks.
Stone, M. (2009). *Yoga for a World Out of Balance.* London: Shambhala.

4

Need of the Hour : Spirituality in Work Life and Family Life

The primary role of an HR manager is to manage people in an organization. This includes selection of the employees and maintaining their efficiencies. With changing time, however, these roles have also changed. What was once the task of selecting employees is today the process of team-based hiring of the best talented employees and holding them back. Not only that, the HR Department is also supposed to tell the employees to follow the organization's culture.

NEED OF THE HOUR

In recent years, there has been a marked increase in dual-career families. Dual-career families or dual-earner families are those in which both the partners of a married couple are working outside. As a result, marital relationships are getting affected both positively and negatively. This is a fact that the income of such couples has gone up but their companionship, husband-wife contact, communication, sex satisfaction, and child care have gone down. As a whole, the outcome is more negativc than positive in many cases because they are having anxieties and stress all the time. Divorce rate is also increasing in such families. There was a time when the female colleagues were agreeing to prepare dishes and male employees making well-coordinated plans. The essence of this kind of understanding between husband and wife was to bring love, peace, and harmony at all levels. But today, there is nothing like "his job" or "her job". As a result, expectations from each other in marriage have changed completely. Since these expectations – who will do what – are not clear, many of the couples are suffering from overload of work and role ambiguity. In such situation, children are the worst sufferers. More income of the family, therefore, cannot solve these problems. Since we cannot go back to the old family system, we need to learn about how to cope with the changed environment and how to maintain a balance between the work life and family life.

Advancement of science and technology has created another problem. Now, there is nothing like "nine-to-five" working hours. Since employees have many methods to work such as e-mails, computers, and cell phones, which enable them to accomplish their work beyond the office hours, employers expect that their employees should work also from their homes. Some of the private organizations have even gone for changing the working hours to "nine-to-nine". This has changed the traditional work culture and has made the jobs extremely stressful. And all these have been done at the cost of family life. According to a survey conducted by the National Life Insurance Company, four out of ten employees are suffering from this kind of problem today and are depending on stress-related medicines. Women, in particular, are facing this kind of problem more than men.

Social change in India, particularly social disorganization we are heading for, has also multiplied our problems. It has destroyed the old social systems and has changed the mindsets of people. We are no more well-organized and coordinated. We have become more and more "individualistic", "competitive", and "aggressive". We do not like to help others; on the other hand, we enjoy finding faults with others. A kind of negative attitude is developing everywhere. We are becoming more and more materialistic and self-centred. As a result, our family systems, which were well-known once for long-term and harmonious relationships, have started breaking. And before breaking, there are all sorts of quarrels and beatings.

All these changes in our society are pressurising the HR managers to think of something new and effective. Some of us have already started thinking on this line and creating conditions so that employees are able to maintain a balance between their work life and family life. We are also encouraging our employees to be team players and realize their potential values while doing their jobs. As noted by Ashmos and Duchon (2000), "...organizations, which have long been viewed as rational systems, are considering making room for the spiritual dimension, a dimension that has less to do with rules and order and more to do with meaning, purpose, and a sense of community." This has led to a new movement which is pleading strongly for bringing spirituality in the workplace. Our experiences say that wherever employers are more concerned with their employees, production is going up. It has been rightly said by Hoffman (2002), "In coming years, we'll surely see scientific validation on the connection between our spiritual well-being at work and our highest productivity involving both mind and body."

WHAT IS SPIRITUALITY?

The root of the word spirituality is "Spirit" which is present in all living beings as a non-chemical or non-molecular fundamental particle. According to *Vedanta*, we are active and alive only due to presence of this particle, called *atman*. Spirituality is thus regarded as a connection with something external to the self, or as an internal experience, or both. In the words of Mitroff and Denton (1999), spirituality is "the desire to find ultimate purpose in life, and to live accordingly." Cavanagh (1999) compared Mitroff's definition to others and reviewed authors who relied heavily on Taoist, Buddhist, Hindu, Zen, and Native American spiritualities. He found that these non-Western perspectives were superior to Western perspectives in integrating personal life, work, leisure, religion, and other aspects of life. This idea has changed many persons and now for them, to be

"Spiritual" means to know, and to live according to the knowledge that there is more to life "that meets the eye", and there is more to do beyond "nine-to-five".

Spirituality has also been defined in terms of spiritual consciousness. Spiritual consciousness is a state of Being where all limiting, conflicting and contradictory ideas, thoughts, feelings, beliefs, circumstances and events blend together and dissolve into love, peace, and harmony. Once we open into it, the things which were beyond our reach like good health, prosperity, successful relationships, etc., become ours as a natural consequence of this new way of being. But for all these, we need to move on a spiritual journey.

Spiritual journey starts with the correct realization that there are three entities in every human being – Body, Mind, and Soul or Spirit – and out of these three; the Soul is the most important one. Body is the perishable structure and the five senses are tools we utilize to carry out the bidding of the mind. Mind is thoughts – our ability to process information and choose right course of action. But Soul is the life-essence that mirrors our human personality and the divine personality, the personality of God. Since soul is permanent and energy source from God, it is the real identity of a human being.

FACTORS WHICH CAN BRING SPIRITUALITY IN OUR WORK AND FAMILY LIFE

In all these years, we human beings have designed the world to have a taste for bodily existence and enjoy the sensuous pleasure. Therefore, our all material creations are manifested for the sense enjoyment of the mind and body. We have also got the idea that this world is like a playground and we should enjoy our life maximum by satisfying our bodily needs more and more. For this, we should try to have another job or business, a bigger house, a new car, and a more loving partner so that we can get more money, more pleasure, more satisfaction, and thereby, more happiness. But what has happened in reality? Many persons in advanced countries have reached a level that leaves no room for any unsatisfied desire; even then, they are feeling unhappy and want to have "more and more". They do not understand that desires are unlimited and there is no end to it. They simply think that making the body and mind happy will make them happy. They fail to realize that as long as they have this kind of materialistic consciousness, they will never come out of it and will feel always hungry, empty, and unfulfilled. We, therefore, need to realize that engaging in the practices that allow us to regain our spiritual consciousness is the ultimate purpose of human life, and not to remain satisfied with materialistic consciousness. Materialistic consciousness is needed only for survival and need satisfaction. Beyond that, it leads to lust, power, anger, greed, and ego consciousness.

Anybody can say that understanding between co-workers at all levels will enhance the willingness among employees to contribute more than just the required skills, and will give them a better sense of purpose and a higher level of satisfaction. But the question is: how to develop understanding among employees. The sense of togetherness and accepting each other, and seeing each other as a valuable partner will not come in one trial. We have to work for it. There are some suggestions given by Marques, Dhiman, and King (2007) which can be followed to make work life more spiritual:

Ethics: Ethics is a crucial element not only for the worker but also for the workplace as a whole, and ultimately for the entire network the workplace operates in. It is a set of concepts and principles that guide us in determining what behaviour helps or harms sentient creatures. In business, ethics is the accepted set of moral values and corporate standards of conduct. It is expected from all involved that they integrate the value into their sense of spirituality.

Truth: Truth is honesty. This is a basic value which all is supposed to maintain for good results. Everyone knows that Mahatma Gandhi was successful in his mission because he followed the truth in both thoughts and actions.

Belief in a Higher Power: When we perceive that there is some higher power like soul, angels, and God, we feel assured of their helps and guidance when we need. They are actually like ministering servants who have direct connections with our souls, minds, and bodies. Even departed souls can also help us if we have love and respect for them.

Respect: Respect is a kind of positive emotion which comes from within for the entire environment including seniors, other people, and objects we use and see around. It creates positive relationships with others through seamless or invisible connections.

Understanding: Understanding is something like agreeing with others and appreciating. It also includes caring and loving behaviour. For survival and success of any organization it is an undercurrent of acceptance and gratitude.

Openness: Openness may commonly mean being receptive and flexible in a work environment. But sometimes it also refers to organizational reciprocity and accessibility in the organization. It is an essential condition for free flow of communication and reduction of barriers.

Encouraging Creativity: This refers to providing opportunities and venues for developing unique skills, and making the best out of every situation. Some people may add to this perspective the necessity of finding creative alternatives or solution to problems.

While considering presence of the above said positive factors, managers should also see that the negative factors like negativity, excessive control, egocentric behaviour, mistrust, dishonesty, strong hierarchy, and backbiting are absent from the organization. Otherwise, positive factors will not be effective.

Similarly, for making family life more spiritual, the couples need to take care of the following rules to maintain love, peace, and harmony in their relations:

- As per the role demands, they should decide in advance "who will do what" with proper understanding.
- In addition to career planning, they also need to plan for a cordial relationship.

- They also need to understand that in India perhaps both of them cannot think of having "careers". One should go for a "career", and the other for a "job".
- They should make use of technological advances for saving time.
- They should make sure that they spend quality time with each other and communicate freely.
- They also need to take care of their other family members, particularly children.
- They need to learn how to enjoy family life and trust each other.

All the couples need to realize that marriage is a sacred bond tied with love between two soul mates. Therefore, every marital relationship should be like a "soul-mate" relationship which should grow and develop like a beautiful flower. This, however, does not happen suddenly or by chance, we have to rather work for it. We have to nurture it and treat it like a valuable resource. It has been rightly said by Springett (2008), "A soul-mate relationship is actually a means of bringing out the best in us and making us more complete and whole over time than we have been before."

REFERENCES

Ashmos, D. P., and Duchon, D., (2000). Spirituality at work: A conceptualization and measure. *Journal of Management Inquiry,* 9(2), 137.

Cavanagh, G., (1999). Spirituality for managers: Context and critique. *Journal of Organizational Change Management,* 12(3), 186.

Hoffman, E., (2002). *Psychological Testing at Work.* New York: McGraw Hill.

Marques, J.; Dhiman, S.; and King, R., (2007). *Spirituality in the Workplace: What it is, Why it Matters, How to Make it Work for You.* Delhi: Macmillan India.

Mitroff, I., and Denton, E., (1999). *A Spiritual Audit of Corporate America: A Hard Look at Spirituality, Religion, and Values in the Workplace.* San Francisco: Jossey-Bass.

Springett, U., (2008). *Soul-Mate Relationships.* NY: Harper Collins Publishers.

5

The Secret behind the Success of Tatas*

TATAS AT A GLANCE

Jamsetji Nesserwanji Tata and his sons were products of an era in which bold and adventurous men made large fortunes by exploiting the scientific discoveries and inventions of the nineteenth and early twentieth centuries. While Jamsetji shared the spirit of entrepreneurship of men like Rockefeller, Krupp, Leverhulme, and Ford, he was of a special breed (Lala, 2004). When he saw that under the exploitation of colonial rule, his country was being bypassed by the industrial revolution, and Europe and America were transforming rapidly, he decided almost single-handed to launch India on the path of modern science and industry. Since he was successful in two textile ventures, many of his contemporaries thought that he would multiply his wealth by adding to his textile units. But he chose the unknown path to give India steel, hydro-electric power, good technical education, and a good hotel. Something had really happened to Jamsetji because much more was to come from his fertile genius. It was really a struggle for his successors to set up a steel plant and get under way the hydro-electric projects at that time. It was also a battle

* This article was co-authored by Dr. Deepa Chatterjee, Senior Lecturer in English, RIMS, Rourkela, Orissa.

to establish a university of science and technology and a hotel for them. But, for Jamsetji, it was a dream project and the key to India's modernization. He proceeded with his steel and hydro-electric projects. He knew that he was 60 and time was running out. The result was, as put by Lala (2004), "India's leap from the Middle Ages to the threshold of the twentieth century." Today, we have about 100 national and international companies of Tata Group working successfully throughout the world. To get some ideas about them, a few examples are cited below:

Tata Steel: Formerly known as Tata Iron & Steel Company Limited (TISCO), Tata Steel is the world's sixth largest steel company, with an annual crude steel capacity of 31 million tonnes. In India, it is known as the largest integrated and profit making steel company in the private sector with consolidated revenue of Rs. 1,32,110 crore and net profit of over Rs. 12,350 crore during the financial year ending 31st March, 2008. Its main plant is located in Jamshedpur (Jharkhand, India) and has about 82,700 people as employees (as of 2007).

Tata Motors: Formerly known as Tata Engineering & Locomotive Company (TELCO), Tata Motors is India's largest commercial vehicle manufacturer — rated among the top six manufacturers in the world. It is also among the top three passenger car manufacturers in the country. Recently, it has designed and manufactured the iconic Tata Nano which is supposed to be the cheapest car in the world – available at approximately Rs. 1,00000.00 (USD 2300.00). In March 2008, it has finalized a deal with Ford Motor Company to acquire their brands Jaguar Land Rover (JLR) business, which also includes Daimler and Lanchester brand names.

Tata Consultancy Services: It is India's largest provider of Information Technology and Business Process Outsourcing Services headquartered in Mumbai. It is interested in areas such as energy, telecommunications, financial services, manufacturing, chemicals, engineering, materials, government, and healthcare. It was established in the year 1968 with F.C. Kohli as its first General Manager. He realized that India's strength lay in its brain power, second to none in the world, and made the TCS a first-rate software engineering and service provider. In 1999, it saw outsourcing opportunity in E-Commerce and related solutions and set up its E-Business division with ten people. By 2004, E-Business was contributing half a billion dollars (US) to TCS. Today, it has more than twenty thousand software engineers and is competing successfully with its rivals, Infosys, Wipro, and Satyam.

Tata Power: Led by a powerful vision, Tata Power pioneered the generation of electricity in India. It has now successfully served the Mumbai consumers for over ninety years and has spread its footprints across the nation. Today, it is the country's largest private player in the sector. Apart from Mumbai and Delhi, the company has generation capacities in Jojobera, Jharkhand and Karnataka. The company made history by signing the shareholders' agreement for construction, operation, and maintenance of a 400 KV transmission line from Siliguri to Delhi with Power Grid Corporation, at an estimated cost of Rs. 1,100 crore. This is the first joint venture company of its kind in India. It has also taken over the transmission construction business of Tata International and has orders worth Rs. 200 crore for the construction of EHV lines.

Indian Hotels: The Indian Hotels Company Limited (IHCL) and its subsidiaries are collectively known as Taj Hotels Resorts and Palaces and are recognized as one of Asia's largest and finest hotel company. Incorporated by the founder, Jamsetji N. Tata, the company opened its first property, The Taj Mahal Palace Hotel, Bombay in 1903. The Taj, a symbol of Indian hospitality, completed its centenary year in 2003. Today, it has more than 60 hotels in 45 locations across India with an additional 15 international hotels in Malaysia, United Kingdom, United States of America, Bhutan, Sri Lanka, Africa, the Middle East and Australia. Spanning the length and breadth of the country, gracing important industrial towns and cities, beaches, hill stations, historical and pilgrim centres and wildlife destinations, each

Taj Hotel offers the luxury of service, the apogee of Indian hospitality, vantage locations, modern amenities and business facilities.

Apart from these, there are about ninety other companies of the Tata Group like Tata Chemicals, Tata Tea, Tata Coffee, Titan, VSNL, etc. which are well known for their performances throughout the world. Now, the biggest question is: why are they doing so well? It is really a very difficult question to answer. However, some attempts can be made to unravel this mystery.

JAMSETJI TATA: A MAN OF COURAGE, VISION, AND ACTION

Jamsetji was born in 1839 in a family of Parsi priests in Gujarat. At the age of fourteen, he came to Bombay and at seventeen he joined Elphinstone College for doing graduation. He had love for literature and liked reading Dickens, Thackeray and Mark Twain. After initial trading ventures in the Far East and Europe, he started in 1868 – at the age of twenty-nine – a private trading firm with a capital of Rs. 21,000. He and his associates obtained a contract to furnish suppliers required by the expeditionary force of General Napier in Abyssinia. The share of his profit was sufficient enough for him to launch his career in textiles. His earlier visits to Manchester had stimulated his desire to manufacture cotton goods. He bought an old oil mill in Bombay in partnership with a few friends, converted it into a textile mill, managed it himself, and within a couple of years made it a going concern. He sold it at a profit after two years. This way in 1874, he floated a company named The Central India Spinning, Weaving & Manufacturing Company with a capital of Rs. 1,500,000 subscribed by himself and his friends. Since then, he did not look back and went on doing one thing or the other. It has been rightly said, that Tata had not put gold into the ground but had put in earth and taken out gold.

When India was recovering from the after-effects of the Revolt of 1857-58, some powerful forces were working to change her and to have a new social consciousness. This awakening of India was two-fold: she looked to the West, and, at the same time, she looked to herself and her own past. Indians were asking themselves: why a foreign power had gained such supremacy over their ancient land. Was it because the culture of the West was superior to Indian culture? Or, was it because modern science and technology gave Europe a lead? Thus, a new class of Indians was emerging which was eager to learn English and benefit from the study of western ways and methods. Jamsetji belonged to this class. When he surveyed the untilled industrial field of India, he perceived the benefits it could gain through science and technology. His clear mind immediately grasped it and spelt out the three basic ingredients to attain it: Steel, Hydro-Electric Power, and Technical Education. Pt. Jawaharlal Nehru, the first Prime Minister of India, has rightly said, "When you have to give the lead in action, in ideas – a lead which does not fit in with the very climate of opinion, that is true courage, physical or mental or spiritual, call it what you like, and it is this type of courage and vision that Jamsetji Tata showed."

CHAIRMEN OF TATAS AND THEIR GUIDING PRINCIPLES

Since Jamsetji was the first Chairman of Tata Group from 1887 to 1904, the Tata tradition was created primarily by him. He sought no honour, no privilege, but only the advancement of India. For him, success or failure was not a major issue. Therefore, he did what was needed to be done at that time. In 1902, five years before the site of the steel plant was finally located, he wrote to his son from abroad of what his dream city of steel should look like: "Be sure to lay wide streets planted with shady trees, every other of a quick-growing variety. Be sure that there is plenty of space for lawns and gardens. Reserve large areas for football, hockey and parks. Earmark areas for Hindu temples, Mohammedan mosques and Christian churches" (Lala, 2004). In his last days, he also urged his cousin and other close family members to carry forward the work he had started: "If you cannot make it greater, at least preserve it. Do not let things slide.

Go on doing my work and increasing it but if you cannot, do not lose what we have already done."

All these ideas have been translated into action by his successors: Sir Dorabji Tata (1904 to 1932), Sir Nowroji Saklatvala (1932 to 1938), J.R.D. Tata (1938 to 1991), and Ratan Tata (1991 to continue). From time to time, each Chairman and Managing Director has been adding something of his own which can be summed up as follows (Lala, 2004):

- Nothing worthwhile is ever achieved without deep thought and hard work.
- One must think for oneself and never accept at their face value slogans and catch phrases to which, unfortunately, our people are too easily susceptible.
- One must forever strive for excellence, or even perfection, in any task however small, and never be satisfied with the second best.
- No success or achievement in material terms is worthwhile unless it serves the needs or interests of the country and its people and is achieved by fair and honest means.
- Good human relations not only bring great personal rewards but are essential to the success of any enterprise.

After being appointed as Managing Director in 1992, Dr. J. J. Irani jotted down his guidelines as follows:

- Develop a personal vision – what do I want to accomplish in life.
- Tell the truth about current reality.
- Do the tough things no one else wants to do.
- Restructure the TOP TEAM, if necessary.
- Build a powerful guiding coalition-management and board.
- Guide the creation of a shared VISION.
- Take the responsibility of being the main change agent.
- Create endless opportunities for two-way communications.

- Create opportunities for innovations in the rank and file.
- Maintain focus.
- Realign HR systems, overcome obstacles.
- Model the desired managerial behaviour – above all maintain CREDIBILITY.
- Preserve the core values of TATAS (and my own).

Ratan Tata, the present Chairman, has also shared his business values as follows (*The Times of India*, 2002):

Integrity: We must conduct our business fairly, with honesty and transparency. Everything we do must stand the test of public scrutiny.

Understanding: We must be caring, show respect, compassion and humanity for our colleagues and customers around the world and always work for the benefit of India.

Excellence: We must constantly strive to achieve the highest possible standards in our day-to-day work and in the quality of the goods and services we provide.

Unity: We must work cohesively with our colleagues across the group and with our customers and partners around the world, building strong relationships based on tolerance, understanding, and mutual cooperation.

Responsibility: We must continue to be responsible, sensitive to the countries, communities and environments in which we work, always ensuring that what comes from the people goes back to the people many times over.

KEY BUSINESS SECRETS OF THE SUCCESS OF TATAS

1. **Planning Ahead for Success:** In the early 1980s, Dr. J.J. Irani, the then General Manger, told J.R.D. Tata: "If we do not modernize the steel plant, in a few years time you and I will be standing outside the steel plant selling tickets to visit a steel museum." This was taken very seriously by the whole

Board. The modernization was implemented from 1988 to 2001. The old machinery was replaced by new ones. This resulted in enhanced production and of making only special steels. By 2003, Tata Steel had the capacity to supply special steel to the whole of India at the price that was near to the cheapest in the world. This made J.J. Irani the Managing Director who proved, "It is people who build companies, not just ideas. For a company to survive for a 100 years, the organization should have at its head the right man at the right time."

2. **First in introducing a Number of Labour Welfare Schemes:** Tata Steel has been the first in introducing a number of labour welfare schemes. Be it eight hours work, workers' provident fund, or handling complaints and grievances, it did much before many of the countries/ governments could think of. The following Table gives a clear-cut idea when it was done by TISCO and when it was done by the Government (Lala, 2004):

	Introduced by TISCO	*Introduced by Law*	*Legal Measure*
Eight-hour Working Day	1912	1948	Factories Act
Free Medical Aid	1915	1948	Employees State Insurance Act
Establishment of Welfare Department	1917	1948	Factories Act
Schooling Facilities for Child	1917		
Formation of Committees for handling complaints and grievances	1919	1947	Industrial Disputes Act
Leave with pay	1920	1948	Factories Act
Workers' Provident Fund Scheme	1920	1952	Employees Provident Fund Act
Workmen's Accident Compensation Scheme	1920	1924	Workmen's Compensation Act
Institute for Training of Apprentices	1921	1961	Apprentices Act
Maternity Benefit	1928	1946	Bihar Maternity Benefit Act
Profit Sharing Bonus	1934	1965	Bonus Act
Retiring Gratuity	1937	1972	Payment of Gratuity Act
Ex-Gratia Payment	1979		

3. **Creation of a New Industrial Culture:** At a time when captains of industry in advanced countries were exploiting their workers, Jamsetji was thinking of welfare of his workers. He cared to give them filtered water, sanitary hutments, cheap foodgrains, medical facilities, provident fund and accident insurance. It was this policy of Jamsetji which resulted in eight-hour day for workers in steel company in 1912 and in J.R.D. Tata's thinking of a company's responsibility beyond obligations to its own workers. In his Keynote address at a Memorial Lecture (1969), he suggested that "...the most significant contribution organized industry can make is identifying itself with the life and problems of the people of the community to which it belongs, and by applying its resources, skills and talents, to the extent that it can reasonably spare them to serve and help them." To put J.R.D. Tata's ideas into action, the Articles of Association of leading Tata companies were amended and social obligations beyond welfare of employees was accepted as part of the objectives of the group. For example, the Articles of Association of Tata Chemicals were altered to state that the company could subscribe to assist or to guarantee money to charitable, benevolent, religious, scientific, national, public, and political or any other useful institutions' purposes.

   What is important is that the concern shown by the management has become today a part of the culture of the workers of different companies. They feel that they belong to the company and it is their responsibility to take care of the surrounding areas as well. As a result, they go to the villages nearby at regular intervals and do their best to help them in various ways. If there is any natural calamity, by and large, all contribute at least one day salary. This amounts to several lakh rupees for a big company. The board of directors of the company either matches the amount given by the staff and workers or gives more. This shows how Tata is not only for business but also for many things beyond business.

4. **Tatas' Functioning:** Like every successful businessman, different Chairmen of Tata Group have been defining and redefining their styles of functioning from time to time. It is a fact that the business started with a single hand but gradually, on expansion, it went on changing in different hands. This way in 1938, when J.R.D. Tata took over as its Chairman, his style of functioning became quite different. He democratized the working of Tatas and became popular as a 'consensus man.' He went on to reveal the secret of his teamwork: "If I have any merit, it is getting on with individuals according to their ways and characteristics. At times it involves suppressing yourself. It is painful but necessary .... To be a leader you have got to lead human beings with affection." When he was asked to define the house of Tatas, he said, "I would call it a group of individually managed companies united by two factors. First, a feeling that they are part of a larger group which carries the name and prestige of Tatas, and public recognition of honesty and reliability – trustworthiness. Each company enjoys its share of the privilege. They use Tata emblem. The reason is, you might say, enlightened self-interest. The other reason is more metaphysical. There is an innate loyalty, a sharing of certain benefits. We all feel a certain pride that we are somewhat different from others."

   For J.R.D. Tata, details and perfection were important considerations. Even at eighty-six, for the exact meaning of a word, he was consulting dictionaries. He never had any interest in making money but he was very meticulous about the use of money and the shareholders' funds. If there was anything of his topmost interest, it was human relations in Tata Steel. As described by Lala (2004), one day when he was seriously ill in 1943, he wrote from his sick bed a thoughtful note: "If we have 50,000 machines, we would undoubtedly have a special staff or a department to look after them ... but when employing 30,000 human beings, each with a mind of his own, we seem to have assumed that they would look after themselves and that there was no need for a separate organization to deal with human problems involved." He wanted the workers to have a say in their welfare and safety, and he wanted their suggestions on the running of the company. The note resulted in the founding of a personnel department. As a further consequence of that note two pioneering strokes of Tata Steel came about, namely, a profit sharing bonus and a joint consultative council. These measures pre-empted any labour trouble and Tata Steel has enjoyed peace between management and labour since then.

CONCLUSION

Like any other business story, Tatas' story is also the story of struggle, anxiety, adventure, and achievement. However, so far success story is concerned; Tatas' story is quite different. It has gone for continuous expansion and achievements. It will be wrong to say that it has not passed through some bad time. It has, and it has also seen some downfalls. But, with proper planning and timely action, it has come out of it quickly and has made satisfactory progress. Even if there was some loss to one company, it was compensated by others. This way, the balance sheet was always in plus. As a result, it went on moving ahead – from one to two, two to three, and so on. Today, it has about one hundred companies. This success story is really unimaginable – not only for India but for the whole world. And making a passenger car (Tata Nano) for rupees one lakh only has created another history. This is the reason why today all are interested to know the secrets of success of Tatas.

From management viewpoint, the above mentioned four business secrets give the scientific explanation. However, these scientific explanations will remain incomplete unless one spiritual clue is added to it. In one word, this spiritual clue is: "Philanthropy" of Tatas. The word "philanthropy" has come out of a Greek word — "*Fil-anthra-pi*" — meaning love of fellowmen. It is not only in giving money to others, as we understand it today, it is also in showing concern for welfare of others. Tata Group has gone for doing both the things from the very beginning. In 1889, Lord Reay, Bombay's popular Governor, said in a convocation address that education could no longer develop if universities remained only examining bodies. He called for "real universities which will give fresh impulse to learning, to research, to criticism, which will inspire reverence and impart strength and self-reliance to future generations." Such advanced learning was not available in India at that time. So in 1892, Jamsetji endowed a fund for the higher education abroad of deserving students. Some of India's early engineers, surgeons, physicians, educationists, barristers, and ICS officials benefited from the endowment. In 1898, Jamsetji decided to set aside fourteen of his buildings and four landed properties in Bombay to establish a university of science. His donation was worth Rs. 30 lakh in those days, equal to over Rs. 10 crore of today. It was half of his entire wealth. Some of his fellow Parsis even regretted that the wealth of their community was being diverted to a scheme from which only a few Parsis would benefit. In reply to them, in an interview Jamsetji spelt out his views on philanthropy as follows: 'There is one kind of charity common among us which clothes the ragged, feeds the poor, and heals the sick and halts. This is patchwork philanthropy. But what advances a nation by lifting up the best and the gifted ones so as to make them of the greatest service to the country is the best charity. I prefer this constructive philanthropy.'

Jamsetji was fortunate in his sons and successors. 'Trusteeship' was a by-product of the desire Jamsetji Tata and his sons had to tackle the needs of the nation. Their wider concern made them look beyond their business interests. It was rightly written in *100 Great Modern Lives* by John Canning (Editor, Souvenir Press, London):

"Probably no other family has ever contributed as much in the way of guidance, industrial development, and advancing philanthropy to any country as the Tatas have to India, both before and since independence."

It can be now safely concluded that Jamsetji Tata had a burning zeal to pitchfork his country among the great industrial nations of the world. His schemes for steel, hydro-electric power and the institute of science were geared to this one aim. So was his passion to train young Indians. Maintaining the same tradition, Ratan Tata, the present Chairman, has rightly remarked, "My successors would never compromise and turn to soft options to meet their ends, and never allow the Tata group to join the growing number of companies in India which have shed their values, forgotten about their integrity, and closed their eyes to maintaining ethical standards. If Mr. J.R.D. Tata was able to uphold the values of the firm and if I have been able to carry on that tradition through my tenure, I hope the future generations in Tatas will recognize these traditions as being critical to the fabric and the fundamentals on which our group was built and grew so successfully for over a century."

NOTE

This article is based on the book, *The Creation of Wealth* by R.M. Lala published by Penguin Books India, 2004.

6

Concept of God and the Power of Prayer and Meditation

God is a word that has interested human beings from time immemorial. Nobody really knows how long human beings have been thinking about God. There are so many theories and abstractions that there would be no way to record them. However, history says that "God" came into being in English language before the twelfth century AD. Since everything on earth – animate or inanimate – had a spirit for ancestors, everything symbolized God. All were true, and all had their unique functions. As societies advanced, gods were conceptualized in all aspects of life, and people began to worship them in a systematic way. All these became essential because people realized that gods and goddesses were playing an important role in their lives. It did not matter whether the god/goddess worshipped was an alligator, a 200 years old tree, a circle of stones, or a Giant Brain. Most people simply had faith in God without questioning Him. They also did not like to seek any proof as they had developed an inherent belief in God. Since they experienced the hands of God everywhere, they worshipped Him or Her in their own ways. Scholars indicate that between 800 BC and 200 AD, the concept of an ultimate reality, *Brahman,* came to being in Hinduism in order to define the greater Truth. It was beyond all concepts and beyond all descriptions. Since then, different religions have believed in the same Creator God in different names as the ultimate reality, and all other gods or goddesses as His reflections.

GOD IN PHILOSOPHY AND SCIENCE

Today, there are many concepts of God. However, each concept believes in something somewhere that has created the Universe with divine intelligence: All is God; God is Great; God is One; God is the Almighty and Supreme; God is beyond Space, Time, and Causation; God includes Everything, Everywhere, All the Time; and many more. From these concepts it is clear that in different religions, God has been conceived as a Supernatural Power. Since this power is invisible, nobody has been able to define Him or Her exactly. Phelan has rightly said that if we cannot measure the outer edge of the expanding Universe, how can we dare to define its Creator? Any definition of God, therefore, must be open ended with a scope to grow. In spite of these limitations, some philosophers and scientists have always tried to know Him and to find out some acceptable proofs for His existence. And, very often, they have cited the following three kinds of arguments to support His existence:

The Causality Argument: Thomas Aquinas (thirteenth century philosopher) was probably the first to use the argument that if every effect had a cause, there has to be an ultimate cause. And that ultimate cause can be nothing but God. He has given the following five arguments to prove the existence of God:

- The chain of causation proves a first cause that needs to be uncaused to end the otherwise endless chain of events.
- The fact of change proves an ultimate agent of change.
- The contingent facts of the world require an ultimate Being.
- The fact of graduation of things as higher and lower suggests Perfected Being at the top of the hierarchy.
- The order and design found in nature suggest a higher Being at the Source.

The Time Argument: Muslim philosophers have argued that if the Universe had a beginning at all, the beginning cannot rest on nothingness but God. The key here is the concept of infinity. Surely, if we have to go back infinitely without arriving at a beginning, there could be a great problem with having arriving at the present moment.

The Design Argument: William Paley (eighteenth century philosopher) concluded that all living creatures are too complicated to have arisen by chance. For him, the Universe was clearly showing direction and an instrument for a goal. Therefore, the Universe must be a product of an intelligent designer. And that designer has to be no less than God. Marilyn Adamson puts the following five straightforward reasons to support his claim:

- The complexity of our planet points to a deliberate Designer who not only created the Universe but sustains it today.
- The Universe had a start – what caused it?
- The Universe operates by uniform laws of nature. Why does it?
- The DNA code informs and programmes a cell's behaviour.
- God exists because He pursues us. He is constantly initiating and seeking for us to come to Him.

Apart from these philosophers and other thinkers, many scientists have also believed in God. For example, for Newton, all the particles which made matter and the forces between them were created by God because they were not a subject to further analysis. Not only that, God had also created the fundamental law of motion and set the whole Universe in motion which continues to run till today, like a machine. That means, whenever scientists failed to explain something further, they attributed this to chance or God. Even Einstein, like Newton and Galileo, had to believe in the fact that a Greater Power had created and maintained the Universe.

GOD IN QUANTUM PHYSICS

Though quantum physics has changed the Newtonian worldview completely, it has established God in its laboratory by supporting His different concepts. For example, to support that God is everywhere all the time, it says that everything in the Universe, including us, is energy, and that energy moves in a circular fashion. At the microscopic level, we are a whirling mass of electrons and energy atoms spinning rapidly. In fact, everything in the Universe is comprised of energy and we are intimately connected with this sea of energy, this sea of whirling electrons. Thus, energy is the sub-atomic particles that in turn make up atoms and finally matter. This energy exists as waves spread out over space and time. Our thoughts, feeling, words, and actions are also different forms of energy. What we think, feel, say, and do in each moment comes back to us to create our realities. Thus, everything is energy in the Universe which is present everywhere all the time. Quantum Physics says further that it is the act of observing an object that causes it to be there where and now we observe it. Since energy exists as waves, when we exercise observation, they become particles localized as a space-time event. And, as soon as we withdraw observation, they become, a wave again. That means, it is the observation, attention and intention which literally create that thing as a space-time event. Perhaps the most awesome implication of quantum mechanics is the possibility that the Universe only functions because it is continually observed by "someone" who never blinks His eyes or sleeps. This is the reason why some people define God as "Self-energetic Awareness."

It is thus clear that no solid object is solid. It is made up of rapidly flashing packets of energy – billions and trillions of packets of energy. They flash in and flash out of that space where the 'object' is. They do not just stay there. When we watch a movie, we just see a person walking across the screen smoothly. Yet, in reality, it is just a film reel with 24 slightly different frames a minute so our eyes do not detect the gap between the frames. Even each of those frames is a composition of billions of light photons flashing at the speed of light. That is what our world is – a rapid flash that causes an illusion of being solid and continuous.

Physicists have also discovered that quantum 'particles' make decisions. They are powered by intelligence. Not only that, they also know instantly, what decisions are being made by other particles anywhere else in the Universe. This synchronicity across space and time is instantaneous. That means, they 'communicate' without taking any time or crossing any space. So, what is the intelligence that powers them? Well, it is the "Mind of the Source" — God. If the Mind of God did not exist, we would not exist. Thus, the Creator God is the power with which we are conscious and the planets, the Sun, the Solar System, the Galaxy, and the Universe are the effects of thinking of the Mind of God.

The latest discoveries ranging from transpersonal psychology and the increasingly important new discipline of science of consciousness, to Quantum Physics also lead to a similar perception that there is a universal field of consciousness. This kind of consciousness cannot be a part of the brain but a part of the mind known as Universal Mind or Superconscious Mind. The consciousness research by transpersonal psychologist, Stanislav Grof confirms that in transpersonal experience, it is possible to transcend the usual limitations of the body, ego, space, and linear time. These experiences are able to bring us into contact with the collective consciousness. Such experiences were for a long time in the case of Eastern traditions of wisdom which is now supported by Western science. Thus, consciousness can be described as a universal field of intelligence underlying the whole of material creation. From all these it can be safely concluded that God exists and exists forever. Since God is a metaphysical reality, for different persons and for different occasions, He exists in different forms. For some, He is the Creator God; for some, the Intelligent Designer God; for some, the Grand Architect God; for some, the Almighty and Supreme God; and for some, the Infinite God. However, as a whole, He is "One", and all others are our abstractions or attempts to understand Him, or to put a "human face" on Him.

REALIZATION OF GOD

We have seen that God is not a physical reality. Therefore, nobody can see Him directly. He can be only realized and experienced. When we look around, we find that, in the Universe, all manifestations are of God and are one with Him. In Him, they live and move and have their beings. This Supreme Intelligence that moves in the earth is manifested in the tiniest molecule as perfectly as in a great planet. How wonderful it will be to realize that there is only one force, one power, one presence, and that is God. This realization, however, will not come to us through any act of our own but through our belief, trust, and faith in Him. If we exercise patience, faith, and the attributes of God, we are bound to have the opportunities to realize Him. We are like an iceberg in the ocean. When we get such opportunities, we melt under the warmth of God's touch and become ocean. Then only we experience God in everything, everywhere, and all the time.

Indian philosophy also says clearly that the goal of human life is self-realization or enlightenment – and that is the real blessing being born in human incarnation. The aim of all mystical traditions is the same. It can even be said of most major religions of the world as each one started off as a path to God or self-realization with specific practices and instructions. There is also the assurance that some others before us have already walked that path and reached the goal. Those people even have left accounts of their journey. Now, it is for us to choose a path and follow its practices and instructions to experience God.

Though there is no 'short-cut' to reach God, the *Bhagavad Gita* suggests the path of *Karma Yoga* as an easy way. It constitutes performing actions as an agent of God – that is without a feeling of expectation of the fruits thereof. However, *Karma Yoga* must be supported by *Bhakti Yoga. Bhakti Yoga* is based on Love and Devotion. The devotee uses the combined energies of all emotions and transmutes them, sublimating them into the highest of all emotions, *Prem* (Love), which is pure, unconditional and divine love. The devotee is, in fact, not even seeking enlightenment or God, he or she is just overflowing with his/her love for God which is the greatest virtue one can cultivate. This path obviously suits and appeals to many because no 'mind and body control' of *Raja Yoga*, and no 'intellectual and intuitive powers' of *Jnana Yoga* are required in this path. Moreover, Love for the creation of God and His all beings always goes on increasing and bringing compassion, tolerance and helpfulness to others.

SPIRITUAL GROWTH

In this material world, we are conscious of the material growth but not of the spiritual growth. We should be equally aware of the spiritual progress that includes both a broadening of understanding of the relation with God, and a definite improvement in capacities for more useful lives. In the human form of life, consciousness *(cetana)* intelligence *(buddhi)*, mind *(manas)*, and senses *(indriyas)* are developed to some extent. But we lack complete spiritual development. Therefore, a human being needs to learn about how to start inner journey to make deeper inquiry *(jijnasa)* – the spiritual inquiry. Einstein has rightly said, "Knowing the plan of God is more important and the rest are details. By this inquiry, *sambandha*, the relationship between the self and God will be established and the pure spiritual knowledge of the self will be understood." Through regular prayer and meditation, such developments can be easily achieved.

PRAYER

Prayer is the concerted effort of our physical consciousness to become attuned to the consciousness of the Creator. It is the attunement of our conscious mind to the spiritual forces that manifest in the material world. It also means entering into the closet of the inner self and pouring the ego out so that the inner being may be filled with the Spirit of God. Thus, prayer is a process of attuning ourselves to reach a higher point of view – of wholeness, of understanding, of oneness with Spirit.

Most of us can recall times when we asked in prayer for something but did not receive. The law of faith says very clearly that whatever you ask in prayer, you will receive, if you have faith. When we pray and ask with faith in Spirit, we bring the creative Forces into play and the results are assured provided there are no other laws in operation at that time to counter our request. For example, we might have created some negative forces which are still in operation. Now, unless those negative forces are resolved, our prayer will not be granted. Therefore, we need to develop full faith in God by sorting out our negative forces first before we start praying.

Faith is an attribute of the soul. As we become cognizant of the physical body through the senses, so we become aware of the soul through the activity of its attributes. We can move step by step to have a complete faith in God. First, we should release our doubts and fears by requesting the Spirit to guide us. As our mind becomes clear from doubts and fears, we start having hopes. Then, as those hopes are realized, we gain confidence in our guidance; and as our confidence grows, we begin to trust. Our experience says that when we truly trust the Spirit within, we get what we want. This is faith which lifts us to the higher dimensions of consciousness and we realize that the infinite power and intelligence of God are guiding us in every aspect of our life. That is why Barnabas says, "Faith is the substance of things hoped for, the evidence of things not seen."

Prayer is also described as talking to God — "communication with God through single-minded devotion." It is an act of thanksgiving, a feeling of surrender, and a reconfirmation of faith in a divine power. Since God urges us again and again to pray to Him, to place our trust in Him, and to turn our motivation to Him, prayer is sure to give us good results. Dada Vaswani maintains that every prayer is answered. The trouble with us is (i) we do not know how to ask God for something, and (ii) how to recognize His answer. Otherwise, He answers every time in our favour in the following four ways:

- The first is 'yes'. We ask for something and He says, "Here it is."

- The second is 'no'. For a good reason, God says, "No, I will not grant your prayer."
- The third is 'wait'. It is as if God tells us that "Time is not ripe for you to receive what you want."
- The fourth is: "Here is something better for you."

Prayer is thus connecting to the divine, recognizing and clearing the *karmic* events of the day, and speaking about our pains and desires. We should be, therefore, honest with ourselves and with God. We should not ask for anything which we do not need, and we should never insist for something. Whatsoever is in our favour, He is sure to give us on His own. Sometimes we insist for something, and then He gives that. But it goes against us in future. Therefore, whenever we are asking for something, we should always add a sentence to our prayer: "Oh God, You give this provided it is in our favour."

MEDITATION

There are three primary levels of spiritual energy: physical, mental, and spiritual. The physical level is the realm of the physical body and ego which includes all those currently in the physical existence as well as those recently crossed over into the spirit realm. The mental level is the realm of the body and soul which includes teachers and spirit guides. The highest level, the spiritual level, includes guardian angels and angels. This level is known as the "Supreme World" – the true plane of God. One can reach all these levels little by little through meditation.

According to Seale, meditation starts with stilling the mind. Therefore, we sit quietly with our eyes closed, back straight, feet flat on the floor or legs folded in a lotus position, and hands resting comfortably on our lap. Then, we take a few deep breaths, allowing our body to relax, and breaths find its own natural, relaxed, and easy rhythm. There is nothing else in our conscious awareness except the breaths. We may notice a great deal of distraction going on in our mind as we attempt to focus our attention solely on our breaths —

inhaling and exhaling. But gradually, distraction goes down. Then, step by step, layer by layer, we go deeper in our consciousness. This process should continue until we realize that we have reached a point of absolute quiet and stillness. This state of mind, however, will be hardly for a few seconds in the beginning. But, gradually, we go deeper and deeper and feel calmer, more centred, and more grounded. We should take our own time to float in this state of mind for a while, and then, when we feel that meditation is complete for now, we should open our eyes. This exercise should continue throughout life. They are not meant to be learnt quickly and easily, because then we would only be learning the lesson on one or two levels of awareness. Life lessons are those on which we continue a lifetime, because we keep going deeper and deeper in our understanding and learning process. In this lifelong journey, a time comes when we realize that we can still our mind for a longer period. At that time, we are unaware of the passing time, and we do not become tired. Our breathing becomes very light and we do not feel disturbed by any noise. Over time, very gradually, the inner light, divine wisdom, vision, and truth awaken in us. This is the time our God enters our heart and starts loving and talking.

Meditation is thus the emptying of ourselves of all that hinders the Creative Force from rising along the natural channels of our physical bodies to be disseminated through the sensitive spiritual centres in our physical bodies. It is arousing the mental and spiritual attributes to an expression of their relationship with their Maker. Only when we are in deep concentration, we know God and realize that He sups with us. It is the spiritual ladder that reaches from the earth to the heavens, from errors to Truth, and from pains to happiness, peace, and enlightenment. It is a magnificent power with which we develop compassion, fearlessness, renunciation, love, and freedom from the cycle of births and deaths. Thus, when we discipline our lives to listen and respond to our souls, we begin to live in alignment with the universal flow, listening to soul as divine self, and creating a life of joy and peace.

REFERENCES

Capra, F. (2010). *The Tao of Physics: An Exploration of the Parallels between Modern Physics and Eastern Mysticism.* Massachusetts: Shambhala.

Reed, H. (1968). *Awakening Your Psychic Powers.* New York: St. Martin's Paperbacks.

Seale, A. (2002). *Intuitive Living.* New Delhi: New Age Books.

Sharan, M. B. (2011). *Metaphysical Realities in Psychology and Management.* New Delhi: Concept Publishing House.

7

The Source of Intuitive Knowledge: Spiritual Communication in Deep Yoga

There are three sources of knowledge: the first is through the five senses, the second is through the intellect, and the third is through the spirit. What we get through our senses and the intellect is known as rational knowledge; and what we get through our spirit is known as intuitive knowledge. Throughout the world, most of us have been trained to have the rational knowledge by using first-two sources because we feel that it is derived from the logical region of mind which functions to discriminate, divide, compare, measure, and categorize. We act from this rational part of the mind and assume that this is the highest form of knowledge. In this way, a world of scientific and intellectual distinction has been created. In Eastern tradition, however, the highest form of knowledge is intuitive knowledge — and not the rational knowledge — because it is derived from the spirit through the intuitive process. The contention is that the ultimate reality or truth cannot be obtained through reasoning or inference because it lies beyond the realms of the senses and the intellect from which our words and concepts are derived. This is the reason why Eastern mysticism advocates that what we are getting through our senses and intellect (rational knowledge) is only relative and approximate. But what we get through our intuitive experience is the 'absolute knowledge.' The *Upanishads* and *Vedas* also differentiate between a higher and a lower knowledge, and associate the lower knowledge with various sciences and the higher with religious or intuitive awareness.

We have seen that the rational knowledge has always been the highest and the only form of knowledge in Western tradition. Recently, however, there has been a change in the mindset of scientists. They have started realizing the limitations of their scientific methods and the knowledge obtained through their intellects. Modern physics is teaching today that every word or concept, clear as it may seem to be, has only a limited range of applicability. Quantum Physics has surprised everyone by saying that the quantum particles make decisions and come to know instantly about what decisions are being made by other particles anywhere else in the Universe. That means, the physicists are accepting today that the particles 'communicate' among themselves without taking any time or crossing any space. This is possible only when we assume that they are powered by the intelligence of consciousness. This kind of consciousness cannot be a part of the human brain but has to be a part of the mind known as Universal or Super-Conscious Mind. And, we know that the Super-Conscious Mind is the soul's mind which has at its disposal all subliminal psychic contents, all those things which have been forgotten or overlooked, as well as the wisdom and experience of uncounted centuries which are laid down in its archetypal organs.

THE INTUITIVE MIND

Different persons define intuition in different ways. For some, it is "the perception of truths, facts, etc., without the conscious use of reasoning"; for some, it is "the immediate knowledge"; and for some, it is the "instantaneous apprehension". Putting all these together and having his personal experience, Swami Omkarananda rightly says, "Intuition is the immediate knowledge of the Absolute, obtained through the eye of wisdom, as opposed to the knowledge of the external objects derived through the exercise of the senses and the intellect. It is a direct vision and apprehension of the Divine Reality underlying the manifested and the unmanifested Universe." Seale is also of the same opinion that intuition is the spiritual energy, which embraces the totality of the universe by acknowledging that there is profound knowledge and wisdom available when we become one with the Spirit or the universal consciousness. It is thus clear that intuition is a meditative process which perceives things without relying on the senses and gives us a kind of creative awareness by interpreting all the informations in a holistic way.

As described by Sri Aurobindo in his book, *The Life Divine*, "Intuition is a power of consciousness nearer and more intimate to the original knowledge by identity; for it is always something that leaps out direct from a concealed identity. It is when the consciousness of the subject meets with the consciousness of the object, penetrates it and sees, feels or vibrates with the truth of what it contacts ...." It leaps out like a spark or lightening-flash from the shock of the meeting. For example, the *Vedas* constitute a body of intuitively gained accumulated knowledge bearing neither date nor any author's name. Individuals who had contributed to this vast fund of knowledge and had written books like the *Bhagavad Gita*, the *Ramayana*, the *Ramcharitmanasa* were all *rishis* who had developed this kind of intuitive mind through the regular practice of yoga. Intuition thus does not work unless one has raised oneself to higher levels of consciousness. This is the reason why the Eastern tradition has been putting the whole emphasis on Patanjali's yoga for developing the intuitive mind or Super-Conscious Mind.

We have wonderful arrangements within us of our body, mind, and spirit. Body is physical whereas mind and spirit are metaphysical. These three entities work together and, therefore, have to work in harmony with each other. Human mind, which is like an internal instrument, is getting the power of consciousness from the soul. This is the reason why *Vedanta* says that it is possible for us to make our conscious mind "Super-conscious" by feeding it regularly with good food (good thoughts and ideas) and by using positive attitude. When we adopt an attitude of faith and acceptance, when we confidently accept and believe that everything that is happening to us is moving us progressively towards the achievements of our goals, our Super-Conscious Mind seems to come alive, like all the lights have been turned on in a room.

According to Seale, when we step into the Super-Conscious or Intuitive Mind through meditation, we are stepping into a realm of which we have no conscious knowledge. This is a realm of imagination where we can function on many levels of awareness at once, and where there are no boundaries or restrictions. Out of these imaginations, by quieting the mind, we come to know finally what information we are "receiving" intuitively from the spirit. This is the way, we gain confidence and trust in our intuitive process, and gain more faith and trust in receiving guidance from the spirit. By intuitive living and regular prayer and meditation, the essence of yoga, we can get even wonderful results as our ancestors and *rishis* did in the past.

DEEP YOGA

Yoga is a systematic way of establishing connections and maintaining balance among the three entities - body, mind, and spirit. In a traditional sense, it is a technique to unite individual *atma* with *Parmatma.* It is an ancient psycho-physical discipline which teaches about how to set aside the conscious mind and have the experiences of the Subconscious and the Super-Conscious or Universal Mind. Credit goes to the Indian sage, Patanjali, who recognized all these about two thousand years ago and wrote a book, *"The Yoga-Sutra"* which described the various aspects of yoga in the following eight limbs: *Yamas* (moral precepts), *Niyamas* (personal observances), *Asanas* (postures), *Pranayama* (control of life force), *Pratyahara* (withdrawal of the senses), *Dharana* (concentration), *Dhyan* (meditation), and *Samadhi* (absorption). These eight limbs have often been likened to a ladder that we climb to reach higher consciousness. We begin by embracing moral precepts and personal observances, then purify and strengthen the body and mind, and finally, we ascend into unification, or *Samadhi.* Central to this process is *Abhyasa* (practice) and *Vairagya* (detachment). Today, it is accepted throughout the world as a pathway to personal enlightenment, a formula designed to take us into unification with our higher Self or God. In short, it is the richest and most complete scientific lifestyle, and spiritual system ever devised by humankind.

There are a number of ways to take yoga off our mats and begin to integrate it into our daily lives. In this context, Bhava Ram suggests the following seven simple and practical steps which must be followed by everyone to begin with and deepen the process:

1. **Deep Breathing:** One should learn how to breathe deeply and fully, in a 3-part yogic breath, first belly, then ribs, then chest, and then exhaling chest, ribs, and belly.
2. **Becoming More Intimate with Nature:** One should learn how to go for a morning walk and appreciate the flowers, bushes, and trees in his neighbourhood or workplace.
3. **Authentic Speech/Silence:** We should make our speech more authentic and from our heart instead of our head. We should recognize that our speech is sacred and the language we choose affects our level of consciousness as well as the consciousness of those who are listening. Along with this, we should also spend more time in silence.
4. **Mindful Eating:** Our body is the Sacred Temple of our Spirit. Therefore, we should try to eat as fresh, organic, and pure food as possible. And we should take time to bless each meal in some silent and simple way.
5. **Material Cleansing:** We should find time to go through each storage area and get rid of everything we don't' need. If we have not used something for more than a year, it is time to let it go.
6. ***Seva:*** *Ahankara* (ego), or the sense of "I-ness" is one of the primary obstacles to yoga. A key to accomplishing this is *Seva*-giving to others without any desire for reward and recognition.
7. **Gratitude and Divine Awareness:** We should recognize that there is a Divine Plan and a Divine Essence permeating

everything. Therefore, we should have gratitude for all experiences, all difficulties, and all challenges.

THE EIGHTH LIMB OF YOGA – SAMADHI (ABSORPTION)

The ultimate aim of Patanjali's system, which is often called *Raja Yoga*, is *Samadhi*. It is the deep absorption in the object of meditation, wherein only the essence of that object, place, or point shines forth in the calm and quiet mind, as if the mind were devoid even of its own form. With Meditation, there is still an observer observing an observed. When the observer becomes extremely absorbed in the process of observing the object, the three collapses such that all there is only awareness in the object. This is when Meditation becomes *Samadhi* – an absorption in God Consciousness. In this state of mind we move from the temporal to the eternal and our soul communicates with other souls and God.

Spiritual Communication

Communication is taking place constantly, all around us as well as within us. We use countless ways to communicate in our lives. Not only human beings, the animals, plants and insects also communicate. We can think of the language and intelligence of dolphins, the migration of birds, and the organization of a beehive. We can also think of how the DNA and RNA in our cells communicate across generations. That means, all animate things communicate.

Perhaps, we don't know that all inanimate things also communicate. According to Dr. Sha, "Everything in the room in which you are reading this book communicates. The company you work for communicates. The car you drive communicates. Mountains and rivers communicate. Mother Earth communicates. They all communicate with each other." That means, we can communicate not only with animate things, but also with inanimate (visible or invisible) things because everything has a soul. This is known as spiritual communication – communication between soul and soul.

There are many kinds of communication which we categorize as spiritual communication. This depends on our own private beliefs about the nature of the unseen. Is it not a fact that at one time or another we have experienced a situation in which we heard a little voice telling or suggesting something to us? There are different explanations for different people for this kind of experience. For some, it is a voice from within; for some, it is from a spiritual entity like soul, angel, or God. Similarly, some persons assume that this information is already stored there on an energy matrix called the non-local intelligence and we have to simply download it into our brain or mind. For some others, however, it is simply a function of the higher self and we just have to learn how to access those answers. No matter which belief one has, each one is an example of spiritual communication.

There are many advantages of spiritual communication. It can serve us for healing, prevention of sickness, and rejuvenation. We can also receive guidance from spiritual communication. There are occasions when we don't have the full information but we have to take decisions. Our decisions will be correct only when we rely on spiritual communication. A manager or a doctor will be successful only when he/she makes use of spiritual communication by seeking guidance from some supernatural power. Otherwise, decisions taken only on the basis of available data, which are always incomplete, may be wrong. Therefore, Dr. Sha is right when he says that soul communication can be applied to benefit any aspect of our life. And, it can be applied anytime anywhere.

RECEIVING GUIDANCE FROM THE SUPER-CONSCIOUS MIND

There are some practical applications of intuition and spiritual communication. One of them is obtaining accurate guidance from the Super-Conscious Mind (Soul's Mind) for ourselves and for sharing with others. Peirce has suggested the following twelve steps for receiving such guidance:

1. **Relax your body:** One should give full attention to the rhythmic body cycles: his breath, heartbeat, electrical vibration, and the vibration of the cells deep within him. He should create a feeling of absolute safety within himself and the environment around him.
2. **Become alert and aware:** One should concentrate on the simplicity of what surrounds him at the moment. He should suspend personal will and notice the presence of divine will within himself.
3. **Align:** One should bring his body, mind, and spirit into perfect balance. Then, he should feel his connection to the heavens (the Father) through the top of his head and move his awareness to the base of his spine and the earth (the Mother).
4. **Attune:** One should affirm his true identity by feeling the qualities of the soul: "I am infinite energy, I am almighty, I am God, I am one with the flow of the nature and grace."
5. **Focus on your need:** One should feel that he has a genuine need which he cannot get without His help.
6. **Ask:** One should make a request to the Almighty for fulfilling his need. He should, however, add to his request that it should be granted to him only when it is in his favour.
7. **Release:** One should have the faith that the Almighty is sure to give him what he wants because He is aware of his genuine need.
8. **Allow the inflow:** One should have the patience to listen to His God. The inflow is bound to give him a hint that his request has been/ has not been granted.
9. **Consciously recognize the answer:** The Source may use various means to deliver His/Her reply. It may come in words, pictures, symbols, etc. One should have the ability to recognize the correct answer.

10. **Record the answer:** One should note it, record it, or speak it aloud to himself.
11. **Feel gratitude:** One should always appreciate and give thanks for His kind help.
12. **Implement:** One should follow and use the information what he receives with complete faith.

HOW TWO SOULS COMMUNICATE

We have seen that out of three entities, the soul is the vital one in a human being because it is our being. It is our inner self, the unseen part of us. It is divine. Unlike the body and mind which are interdependent, it is a different entity, separable from the body. Therefore, it departs from our physical body upon death. Its responsibility, in part, is to guide the person's thinking, feeling, and will to determine and fulfil his/her life's purpose.

In the world of Quantum Physics, all that exists is ultimately energy, and the way in which energy manifests into recognizable form depends on its vibrational frequency. High frequencies are more effective transmitters than low frequencies, but they become less recognizable to the human senses. Matter can be seen as energy functioning at much lower frequencies. This energy of quantum physics has a telepathic effect among atomic particles which express through their rotary action. It is there that the patterns of psychic energy and the patterns of physical processes become 'One'. This 'One' in *Vedanta* is known as consciousness which is spread across time and space. This is the way two souls communicate with each other instantly. *Rishis* got intuitive knowledge through this process of spiritual communication. If we want, we can also get it by following the same path of deep yoga and spiritual communication.

REFERENCES

Peirce, P. (2000). *The Intuitive Way.* New Delhi: New Age Publications.

Ram, B. (2010). *Deep Yoga.* New Delhi: New Age Publications.
Reed, H. (1968). *Awakening Your Psychic Powers.* New York: St. Martin's Paperbacks.
Seale, A. (2002). *Intuitive Living.* New Delhi: New Age Books.
Sha, Z.G. (2008). *Soul Communication.* Toronto: ATRIA Books.
Sharan, M.B. (2011). *Metaphysical Realities in Psychology and Management.* New Delhi: Concept Publishing Company.

8

The Psychodynamics of Miracles

The term "miracle" has been derived from the old Latin word, "miraculum" which means "something wonderful". It is "an extraordinary and astonishing happening that is attributed to the presence and action of an ultimate or divine power". This cannot be explained by the ordinary law of nature. A reported miracle excites so much wonder that it requires, as its cause, something beyond the reach of human action and scientific explanation. Sometimes it also refers to the action of a supernatural being who is not a god or goddess. Such intervention is attributed to the direct involvement of a deity or a "miracle worker" who is regarded as a saint or a superhuman with exceptional dedication and nearby magical resources. Combining all these characteristics together, the philosopher David Hume rightly defines it as "a transgression of a law of nature by a particular volition of the deity, or by the interposition of some invisible agent."

According to many religious persons, miracles are gracious and mighty works of God that display His unique power and dominion over all creation, including life and death. They are "gracious" because God in His mercy chooses to reveal Himself supernaturally by overruling, suspending, or modifying the ordinary course of nature to interact with mankind. Such direct interventions are, however, occasionally in rare situations. Otherwise, many times He does the same thing by empowering His messengers like Jesus, Sri Sai Baba,

Lord Buddha, Sri Ramakrishna Paramhamsa, Sri Swami Sivananda, and so on.

Whatsoever the circumstances might be, miracles always symbolize a different kind of reality – breaking through the walls of our everyday experience. As noted by Miller, for religious persons, such miracles represent proofs for divine intervention in earthly affairs; for skeptical, they are hoaxes or misinterpretations of mundane phenomena; and for those who waver between faith and disbelief, they suggest that something good or bad is going to happen. Its metaphysics is thus aligned more with traditional Eastern mysticism than with Western religion.

HOW MIRACLES WORK

We all have experienced some kind of "miracles" in our life at one stage or the other – it could be getting something unexpected, seeing a cancer patient surviving beyond hope, escaping a serious accident, or being unexpectedly successful in a job. In each case, we have tried first to analyze the happening logically but we have failed in finding out its cause. Therefore, we assume that it was due to some chance factor (unknown factor), or due to a deity or due to the wish, blessing or grace of God. Whatsoever it might be, we all need to learn about how to receive the miracle power from God.

For this, we must recognize first that miracles are not just "hit and miss". They are governed by the laws of God which can be tapped by having faith in Him and by understanding His way of functioning. God is certainly so powerful that He can perform the miracles Himself but generally He does them through His messengers by empowering them to do so. Only in exceptional cases He does them Himself. We, therefore, should not think that the best way to get miracles is to convince God to do them for us. We are supposed to do our *karmas*/duties with all honesty and sincerity and pray to God for His grace. As per His nature, He is bound to grace and give the results of our *karmas* in accordance with the *karmic* law. His Kingdom operates under consistent laws. He does not do one thing this time and another thing another time. He created the Universe and put everything around us in order. He is, therefore, the same forever and for everyone. It has been rightly concluded by Jordan Seng that "God routinely partners with us to get things done in the world. He reveals truth, but we have to preach it. He offers salvation, but we gather in. He shows mercy, but we serve the poor. Supernatural ministry works the same way: he is the source of the power, but *we* lay on hands or speak commands that the power might flow to others."

In today's world, we often demand quick results. We want to microwave our lives so that we need not wait at all. Laws of *karma* (or of God), however, operate like a slow cooker. They test our patience and then only give the results, including miracles Therefore, *The Bhagavad Gita* rightly says that we are supposed to do our *karmas* with full commitment and devotion without expecting any results. Then only we can get good results or perform miracles by the grace of God.

THE SUPERNATURAL PEOPLE

It is a fact that all physical bodies are developed in accordance with the natural laws. However, different people are born with different souls (subtle bodies) – each with its own desires, own unconscious motivations and tendencies – and they remain as germs of life. These germs of life contain vital forces, sense physical and mental powers, and ethereal particles of matter. Therefore, as suggested by Dr. Giorgio, the natural laws of mind and spirit go beyond the world of Newtonian physics and move into the realm of quantum physics. Thus, those who identify themselves with physical body, remain in the physical world with limited mind of "mortal consciousness". But those who identify themselves with Infinite Spirit, they develop "spiritual consciousness", merged with the ocean of Love, Power, and Wisdom. Such people are known as the "spiritual people" or "God-Realizing People." When these supernatural people are in the state of "spiritual consciousness", supernatural things including miracles appear spontaneously without asking for them. This is the reason why for *saints, yogis* and *rishis,* there are no miracles.

There are also many people — spiritual seekers – who go around "seeking" this state of spiritual consciousness. But it is not something to "seek" but to accept it and live in that state of consciousness. Dr. Giorgio has rightly said, "Seeking it is pretty much like a fish in water, swimming madly around trying to figure out where is water."

There are many ways and methods of practice to get into the correct mindset of spiritual consciousness. Even for those who are for mortal consciousness, it is possible to change the three quantum states of mind: from ordinary mind to extended mind, and from extended mind to extra-ordinary mind. Many of us are working generally with the first state of mind, and have ordinary or sensory perceptions including illusions and hallucinations. But there are occasions, we also work with the second state of mind, and have extra-sensory perceptions like telepathy and precognition. At the same time, there are some persons who work with the third state of mind, and have extra-ordinary perceptions. Scientists and creative persons get something new only in this state of intuitive mind. Since *Rishis* and *yogis,* through *"abhyas"* (practice) and *"vairagya"* (detachment) always live in this third state of mind (extra-ordinary mind), they spontaneously have extra-ordinary perceptions. This state of extra-ordinary mind is known as superconscious or universal mind, or, as described above, spiritual consciousness. It is, therefore, possible to reach the third state of mind, and live in that state through the regular practice of yoga, particularly through concentration, meditation, and absorption as described in the *Yoga-Sutra* of Patanjali.

HOW TO GET SUPERNATURAL POWER

It is one thing to accept that the miracles happen; it is another thing to know why they happen only through the supernatural people; and, it is still another thing to understand how to develop the supernatural power. The above discussion makes it clear that the miracles happen and happen through the supernatural people. Now, the third part is to be answered: How to get supernatural power from God ?

Man was created not only to remain confined with his natural abilities, ordinary mind, reasoning, and the knowledge gained through five senses and the intellect but to go beyond that. Unfortunately, many of us have not been trying to go beyond because we have been told that the scientific knowledge gained through the five senses and the intellect (i.e., rational knowledge) is the highest form of knowledge. Eastern tradition, however, has been teaching from the very beginning that the intuitive knowledge – the knowledge gained through the spirit – is the highest form of knowledge, and not the rational knowledge. Recently, we have come to realize our mistakes and have started obtaining the intuitive knowledge through the Spirit. As a result, we are looking today for God's supernatural power so that we can walk closely with Him.

When we examine the life history of supernatural people, we get some insights into it. First of all, we find that all such people had firm faith in God. Secondly, all were hard workers in their respective fields. Thirdly, they were not for themselves but for others. Fourthly, they all believed in simplicity, honesty and sincerity. Fifthly, they all practiced prayer and meditation and were willing to make sacrifices for others and serve the needy persons. Mahatma Gandhi, for example, believed in *Satya* (truth) and *Ahinsa* (non-violence), Mother Teresa in sacrifice and self-less service to the poor, Swami Vivekananda and Swami Sivananda in increasing the power of concentration. We, therefore, need to develop these basic qualities first to get into the supernatural power.

Summarizing all these, Jordan Seng has tried to explain the process of developing supernatural power through his concept of *"Power Equation."* He says that the power equation is combined amount of *authority, gifting, faith,* and *consecration* which gives us the supernatural power. If one wants to heal the sick or cast out demons, he/she has to increase his/her spiritual power. As we need more power to do something difficult or adventurous, we need more power to do miracles by increasing our amount of authority, gifting, faith, and consecration. These four factors, though related, are independent factors. They are also known as variables because they vary in their amounts in different persons. It will be wrong to assume that by increasing only one variable – say faith — we can get the supernatural power. We need to increase all the four components to inherit supernatural power and do the miracles.

Authority: Authority can be defined as our right to wield the power of God. However, authority should not be considered as an entitlement in the kingdom of God but as a privilege. Therefore, in no case, it should create the feelings of authority and dominance because they lead to the feelings of ego. It should rather create the feelings of submissiveness and obedience to God because they give us the authority to wield His power. That means, those who are most obedient to God have the most power to do supernatural things because they get His mercy and blessings easily. We, therefore, should always look for chances to obey God and for ways to exercise obedience in the moment of doing supernatural things.

Gifting: It is said that the supernatural people are "gifted" persons. Each one of us is gifted to do something special easily and comfortably which others cannot do with that ease. Some are very good dancers, some are very good painters, and some are very good in having deep concentration from childhood. All such cases are known as gifted persons. Similarly, in the world of doing miracles, some are gifted to drive out demons, some are gifted to cure cancer and other serious patients, and some are gifted to treat snake-biting cases. Even in day-to-day life, we find that some are known as very good teachers, some are very good in mathematical calculations, and some are very good in handling computers. These qualities are something like inborn qualities (gifted qualities) which are not due to learning or experience.

In many cases, these qualities are manifestations of the Spirit – specially equipped by God in certain areas. Different *Bible* passages and other religious books list many examples of such gifts that God gives supernaturally — prophecy, words of wisdom, healing, discerning of spirits, interpretation of tongues, teaching, leadership, craftsmanship, and many more. According to Jordan Seng, we get these gifts in two ways: (i) by praying to God to give as per our needs; and (ii) by borrowing from those who already possess them. The second way is easy to have because we simply need to identify with these persons through our love, respect, and appreciation.

Faith: Faith is an attribute of the soul. When we pray or ask the Spirit to help us with full faith, we bring the creative Forces into play and get the results. We, therefore, need to develop full faith in God by sorting out our all negative forces operating at that time. For this, we need to move step by step. First, we should clear our doubts and fears by requesting the Spirit to guide us. When our mind becomes clear from doubts and fears, we start having hopes. When the hopes are realized, we gain confidence in our Spirit's guidance. As our confidence grows, we begin to trust the Spirit within. Our experience says that when we truly trust the Spirit, we get what we want. Thus, this is the faith which lifts us to the higher dimensions of consciousness and makes us realize that God is guiding us in every aspect of our life. Barnabas has said rightly that faith is the substance of things hoped for, the evidence of things not seen.

God's ultimate aim is to encourage us to trust His love. Therefore, God is always willing to empower us to do miracles provided they are for good cause. That means, for healing, deliverance, revelation or provision, supernatural power is easily available. Sometimes, a healer is not successful because he/she has some selfish interest or the patient does not have full faith in the healer. We, therefore, should maximize first the pure feelings of faith in both the parties involved. That is why coaches tell athletes to focus their minds on the game before they start playing the game, to ignore the fears, and to embrace the confidence.

Consecration: The word "consecration" literally means "to associate with the sacred." Persons, places, or things can be consecrated. Therefore, the term is used in different ways by different persons. For many persons, however, it is the solemn dedication to a special purpose or service, usually religious. The Church has always advocated "consecrating yourself to Jesus Christ through the Blessed Virgin, the perfect model of discipleship." It is thus a concept that refers to the way in which we dedicate ourselves to the things of God through specific sacrificial acts. Typically, it involves giving up our normally acceptable ties to worldly, fleshly things in order to make space for higher spiritual power. In simple words, it is getting fully ready by purifying our mind and body to accept God's will for our lives. It is the will of God that rings our bell and calls us out. Somewhere there is a soul that needs us and calls us to feed the hungry, to give water to thirsty, and to help people in troubles without any expectations of praise or rewards. It has been rightly said that we cannot make a sacrifice that costs us nothing and for heaven to gain space in us, the world must lose.

Fasting is also considered in Hindu religion a great consecrating exercise because it involves forsaking what is earthly in pursuit of heavenly purpose. Any earthly desire can be an object for fasting: food, sleep, sex, and other comforts. This is the reason why *saints, yogis,* and *rishis* decide to lead a different kind of life to get spiritual power and do miracles.

There is another condition of consecration: *humility.* In the name of supernatural power, we should not think of doing only great things. Ninety-nine per cent of the works which bless us and advance our supernatural power come from our normal duties – maintaining good family relationships, personal associations, and neighbourhood helpfulness. Consecration, therefore, must be a spirit in us – a spirit of love for everyone. When this is the motto, we shall never lack guidance in finding the duties of our consecration. One day's work leads to another; one duty opens the way to another. We are never shown divine maps with all the course of our lives projected on them – but we shall be shown always the next duty, and then the next.

REFERENCES

Giorgio, L. D. (2012). In *Develop Supernatural Powers.*
http://www.deeptrancenow.com/supernatural.htm
Hume, D. (2011). In Stanford Encyclopedia of Philosophy.
http://plato.stanford.edu/entries/miracles/
Miller, D. P. (2008). *Understanding A Course in Miracles.* Berkeley, California: Celestial Arts.
Seng, J. (2012). *Miracle Work.* Lexington, KY: Symbolic Books.

9

The Ultimate Purpose of Human Life: Spiritual Consciousness

We all have basic needs for food, shelter, and physical well-being. But when these basic needs are satisfied, getting more food, more money, a bigger house does not produce increasing happiness or enduring satisfaction. At this time, some of us start thinking why God created this world, and what is the purpose of human life. To get the answer, some decide to follow the spiritual path. This spiritual journey, however, can sometimes begin in a person in a mysterious way — a profound thought may suddenly appear in the mind of a person, one may read a great book, one may meet a great saint and get a word of wisdom from him or her, one may have a meaningful glance, or a miraculous experience. Thus, any motivational and gracious happening can change our life and compel us to start a spiritual journey.

The world is obviously designed to have a taste for bodily existence and enjoy the sensuous pleasure. Therefore, all material creations are manifested for the sense enjoyment of the mind and body. As a result, this has become a playground for those who want to enjoy this kind of life and do not want to come out of such world of *maya* or illusion. But, a time comes when some persons suddenly come to realize that the pleasure of the mind and senses is temporary and limited. It does not really satisfy the soul, which is the real identity of a human being. Then, they start looking for how to get out of this materialistic world and confusion. Lord Buddha is the best example of having this kind of experience and moving on the spiritual path suddenly.

In Western and other advanced countries, many people have reached a level of comfort that leaves no human needs unsatisfied. Even then, they seem to be suffering from "more and more" disease. They think that by getting another job or doing another business, a new house, a new car, a more loving partner, they would get more money, more pleasure, more satisfaction, and thereby, more happiness. But, since unlimited desires go on and on, they never feel happy and satisfied with what they have. Today, many of us are suffering from this kind of problem also in developing countries including India. We think that making the body and mind happy is the ultimate goal of life. We fail to realize that when we are covered by the physical body with a materialistic consciousness, our desires become polluted with lust, anger, greed, and foolishness. As a result, we always feel hungry, empty and unfulfilled although we have everything we wanted. We, therefore, need to realize that engaging in the practices that allow us to regain our spiritual consciousness is the ultimate purpose of life, and not to remain satisfied with materialistic consciousness.

Spiritual consciousness is a state of Being where all limiting, conflicting and contradictory ideas, thoughts, feelings, beliefs, circumstances and events blend together and dissolve into love, peace, and harmony. Once we open into it, the things which were beyond our reach like good health, prosperity, successful relationships, etc., become ours as a natural consequence of this new way of being. However, opening into spiritual consciousness does not happen overnight. It takes a lot of time and energy, and substantial practices to reach the highest level. Some persons may say that the regular practice of yoga and meditation may help in increasing concentration, awakening inner peace, and bringing the mind under control. But, for True Success and True Spiritual Consciousness, it is not enough and we need to start a spiritual journey.

SPIRITUAL JOURNEY

Spiritual journey starts with the correct realization that there are three entities in every human being – Body, Mind, and Soul – and out of these three Soul is the most important one. Body is the perishable structure and the five senses are tools we utilize to carry out the bidding of the mind. Mind is thoughts – our ability to process information and choose right course of action. And Soul is the life-essence that mirrors our human personality and the divine personality, the personality of God. Since soul is permanent and the energy source from God, it always intends and attempts to return to God. Elizabeth Prophet rightly says, "God intends for each soul to return to Spirit and live forever in the divine consciousness as an individualization of the God flame. God is one, but he chooses to make from his oneness single drops of light, individual sons and daughters – all part of his oneness yet distinct and unique."

This is really a grand design of God – a design so exact that at the moment of conception the embryo automatically inhabits all such genes which are suited to the specific soul for its evolution through the cycle of life and death. By this evolution process, the soul reaches the level one day which enables the soul to merge with God from where it came. This level for liberation of the soul (the highest level) is possible only in human life and that also only through spiritual journey because spirituality is able to sustain a working relationship with God. It really does not matter what we call that God – *Ishwar, Allah,* the Higher Self, the Inner Light, Buddha, or something else. It is possible for each one of us to get in touch and stay with God through the process of spirituality. This is, however, not an easy task. It is like climbing on a mountain which has many ways to reach the summit of being. And each way up to the mountain gives us a different experience and perspective of God. According to Elizabeth Prophet, the following keys can help us in climbing the mountain:

1. **Forgive Yourself:** All of us are human beings and are

committing mistakes almost every day for which we are not happy and proud. We should forgive ourselves for the mistakes and *karmas* with a promise that we shall not commit the same in future. God is so kind that He pardons us. We should keep in our mind that balancing *karma* is a joyous path because we are paying our *karmic* debts fully and finally. It is similar to how we feel when we pay all our bills at the end of each month. Therefore, by forgiving ourselves, we feel relaxed and free from all the guilt feelings.

2. **Forgive Others:** We should also forgive others — friends, enemies, and all those who have done something wrong with us. When we forgive them and send love to them, we make ourselves free from entanglements of this life and the previous lives. We should not forget that we can achieve harmony with all parts of the psyche only through the mercy of forgiveness – by forgiving ourselves and by forgiving others.
3. **Make Friends in Heaven:** God created angels before us so that they can take care of us. They are ministering servants who tend our souls, minds, and bodies. They help us as and when we feel helpless and ask for help. They protect, guide, strengthen, heal, comfort, teach, and warn us. Even departed souls are able to help us provided we have love and respect for them. This is the reason why we believe in one God but many angels. Hindus, for example, believe in *Saraswati* for *vidya* (knowledge) *Laxmi* for *dhan* (wealth), *Hanuman* for *bal* (strength), and so on. Since time and space is not a problem for the angels or departed souls, they are available everywhere all the time. We simply need to learn how to take their help.
4. **Learn While Your Body Sleeps:** While we are sleeping, our souls have the opportunity to travel in the subtle body to the retreats of the ascended masters in the heaven-world. They are able to have direct contact with the departed souls and the angels. We, therefore, need to learn how to surrender

and pray to the departed souls and angels for help. This, however, happens only when we go to our beds with peace in mind and intention to get the answer for a particular question from the soul.

5. **Be Aware of the Not-Self:** Not-self is the darker or negative side of the mind which interferes with positive thinking. It may be bad habits, negative thoughts or ego. Unless we put them off, we cannot make progress in our spiritual journey. Is it not a fact that every once in a while, we catch ourselves in a vibration or mood that we can hardly believe is native to us? We become suddenly angry, jealous or feel intense dislike or hatred for someone. And then, all of a sudden, they go and we become normal. We, therefore, need to take care of these negative factors (not self or ego) because they come on the way of taking correct decisions in social interactions.
6. **Work on Your Psychology:** We have strengths in our personality as well as weaknesses. Therefore, when we take a decision to move on spiritual path, we suffer from doubts and suspicions. Unless we control and overcome the obstacles coming on the way, we cannot make progress. It is a fact that moving on the spiritual path is not an easy task because our whole lifestyle changes and we have to make many-many sacrifices. The life of a saint, for example, is entirely different from the life of a common person. For this reason, it is important to work on one's own psychology so that the person goes on making progress without any regrets. For success on spiritual journey up to meeting with the Higher Self or God, we have to take a firm decision to move on and on in spite of having all sorts of difficulties on the way.
7. **Talk with God:** Talking to God is through prayer – both devotional and invocative. Devotional prayer is surrendering to God unconditionally; and Invocative prayer is requesting God for help with full faith in Him. Elizabeth Prophet has

> rightly said, "Prayer is not just a prescribed set of devotions and petitions to God. It is a profound communion wherein we speak with God from the depths of our soul." In reality, it is a conversation in which we only just do not reach out to God but God also reaches out to us with guidance, comfort, direction, and help. It is like "an intimate sharing between friends". Sometimes, as it happens in the case of friends and families, this intimate relationship and sharing between God and devotee may get broken due to communication gap. We, therefore, need to be careful about it, and not to be disappointed.

In short, we can say that when we recognize why we are here and how we got where we are today, the paradoxes of life become much more significant, and meaningful. Once we see that our life is not an isolated segment in time but as part of a continuum, our perspective changes. Every today is a part of the larger creative plan for our soul to ascend back to God. We, therefore, need to go on changing and changing till we become free from the rounds of *karma* and rebirth.

Materialistic consciousness may give us more money, better career, and name and fame, but not love, peace, and harmony. The reason is: it leads to ego consciousness. The ego is a collection of strategies devised by our own mind in response to various experiences in our past. Unfortunately, the old strategies collected by the ego do more harm than good by creating a deceptive sense of a separate and independent "self". This "self-centred" self keeps a person preoccupied with the endless chatter and turmoil of unnecessary fear, anger, and temptation for the whole life. For example, our fears and anger are often only knee-jerk reactions, caused by our ego's projections of past events, which tend to distract us from truly experiencing the wonders of the present moment and dealing with all of life's situations in a loving and kind manner. We, therefore, need to treat ego as an enemy and the biggest obstacle on the way of spiritual journey. This must be suppressed, resisted, crushed, overthrown, or killed. But, at the same time, we should remain cautious about the fact that the feeling of "overcoming the ego" should not add to ego consciousness. Otherwise, the true purpose of spiritual journey will be defeated. David Mutchler has rightly said, "Before you sow the seeds that will grow into Spiritual Awareness, it will first be necessary to till the soil to ensure the seeds take root. The best way to do this is to learn to respect your ego and thank it for all it has done for you. It has gotten you this far in life, which counts for a lot."

GOING BEYOND THE EGO

To go beyond the ego — by moving out of the realm of ego consciousness and entering into the realm of spiritual consciousness – David Mutchler has suggested the following eight steps to be remembered by the acronym LOVE LIFE in which each letter stands for one of the eight steps:

1. **Look For Ego:** Excessive preoccupations with "I", "me", "mine", "my thoughts", "my wants", "my opinions", "my preferences", "my needs", etc., lead to over reactions to situations which create suffering for everyone involved and greatly limit his/her ability to enjoy either the beauty of life or the wonders of the Divine Presence. We, therefore, need to become conscious of our own ego. The moment we start doing so, we rise above ego, which automatically puts us in the realm of Spirit. The purpose is to pay attention to our thoughts, feelings, and behaviours and note what we did wrong, and what we should do now. We should always keep in mind that our limited self is like a wall separating us from the Self of God. God is as far away from us as that wall is thick. The wisdom and justice of God are within us, and yet they are far away under the covering of the veil of the limited self.

2. **Own Your Ego:** Owing one's ego is acknowledging that it belongs to him or her. It is opening oneself to a negative or uncomfortable situation that exists inside without attempting to protest or deny the fact of its existence. Many religions teach about how to annihilate the ego or kill the ego. But it is not possible. It is the ego which teaches us how to survive in the materialistic world. It gives us self protection and self concern and guides us how to meet our basic needs for food, shelter and physical well-being. But beyond that it is unable to give us enduring happiness and satisfaction. And, for that, we need to come out of it and follow the spiritual path. There are occasions when we are under ego's spell and commit mistakes. We also want to regret and apologize for those mistakes because we know that the apology will make us free and help us in moving beyond the ego in Spirit Consciousness.
3. **View Your Ego:** "Looking" for ego is different from "viewing" it. Looking for is becoming aware of ego that it exists. But viewing it is how it manifests itself in every aspect of our life. In every individual, ego develops in the same way – as a separate and deceptive independent "self". As a result, all of us are selfish in nature. But, ego does not manifest itself in the same way in every individual. People define themselves differently and, therefore, develop different self-images. Some are worthy, some are worthless; some are athletic, some are weak; some are honest, some are hard working; and so on. In whatsoever way we develop our self image, we find that it is troublesome. It carries our identity to extreme behaviours to remain superior to others. These extreme behaviours lead us to all sorts of suffering. We, therefore, need to learn about how to change our ego so that it can lead to freedom, happiness, and love.
4. **Examine Your Options:** It has been rightly said by David Mutchler that our Spirit is like the wind that blows where it

wishes, and our ego is like a giant concrete wall that blocks and disrupts Spirit from its freedom of movement. We, therefore, need to remove one by one all the blocks from the wall. With the removal of each block, our Spiritual Consciousness grows. And, the more it grows, the more we are happy, peaceful, and productive. After knowing about the ego and its negative role, we start examining objectively all the options which led to bitterness, anger, disgust, or resentment. We then decide to choose the correct option. The moment we start thinking of a correct option, the Spirit takes over and helps in choosing the correct one. This is a wonderful experience filled with joy and peace of mind because we realize that we are in harmony with our life and all the burdens which we were carrying have been lifted. This state of mind is known as intuitive mind and all the decisions taken by this mind are known as intuitive judgements. Developing this kind of intuitive mind, however, takes time. But we should not get impatient. Growing in Spiritual Consciousness is bound to give us one day the intuitive mind and the intuitive judgements which are always correct.

5. **Listen to the Silence:** Silence is one of the most powerful experiences of *rishis* and *yogis*. They say that it disconnects us from the ego or materialistic world and connects us with Spirit. They also say that we can listen to God only in silence. According to Deepak Chopra, "Silence is the great teacher, and to learn its lessons you must pay attention to it. There is no substitute for the creative inspiration, knowledge, and stability that come from knowing how to contact your core of inner silence." But the modern world we are living in today is full of noise. Many of us spend time sitting in front of a TV watching all sorts of programmes - fighting, killing, beating drums, singing vulgar songs, dancing almost naked, and so on. The same is true with the newspapers – full of

bad and dirty news. In addition to all these, we also have information assault everyday through e-mail, junk mail, magazines, and the increasing number of hours in surfing the Internet. David Mutchler has rightly pointed out, "Having that much information around all day, everyday overloads us and enhances ego's sense of security by leaving little room for the silence in which we would otherwise be able to experience our true Spiritual nature." We, therefore, need to realize that true contentment or full concentration is possible only when our mind is at peace or rest. This stillness of mind, however, should not be taken as a dead space. It is vibrant and dynamic, and it allows us to be open to intuition, creativity, spirituality, and God.

6. **Invite Change:** Change is a continuous and never-ending process. Therefore, nobody can stop it. Its direction, however, can be moulded. But for that, we should be fully aware of its consequences. Many times, its consequences are motivated by external factors known as rewards and punishments. Such outer-directed motivators are ego-oriented. At the same time, there are some inner-directed motivators which are Spirit-oriented. Ego-oriented motivators are temporary, painful, power based, and status related. On the other hand, Spirit-oriented motivators are ever-lasting, love based, purposeful, and fulfilling. David Mutchler, therefore, rightly says, "...before you attempt to make any changes, it will first be necessary to make a conscious decision to get beyond the ego and focus on becoming more Spiritually oriented." Acting from spiritual perspective, anybody can see that he or she has become less critical, happier, more tolerant, more helpful, and more understanding.
7. **Feel the Moment:** Present is more important than the past or future because we learn from the past and plan for the future. All these we do with the help of our memory which

is always in the present. For memories, therefore, there is no past, present, and future. Since ego consciousness is time-bound, we live in the anxieties and worries thinking of the past and imaginary "what ifs" of the future – what if I lose my job, what if I do not get promotion, and what if I get cancer. Unfortunately, many of us have learnt to remain preoccupied with a past and a future that does not exist in the present. We, therefore, need to realize that it is the ego which is promoting our negative thinking and imaginary fears. If we learn to live in the present, we shall be free from a hodgepodge of painful memories and anxiety-ridden anticipation. In the words of David R. Hawkins, "Presence is silent and conveys a state of peace. It is infinitely gentle and yet like a rock. With it, all fear disappears, and spiritual joy occurs on a quiet level of inexplicable ecstasy. Because the experience of time stops, there is no apprehension, regret, pain, or anticipation. The source of joy is unending and ever-present."

8. **Express Your Love:** The key factor of Spiritual Consciousness is love. Love has different meanings for different persons. In English dictionary, it has more than twenty definitions. However, in Greek, as described by David Mutchler, there are five such words which take care of all the twenty: "*Apne*" means having a general affection; "Eros" means passionate love including sex; "Philia" means brotherly love including loyalty to friends or any other person; "Storge" means a natural affection to describe relationships in the family; and "Thelema" means showing love for a profession. Spiritual love, however, is more than all the five put together. It is pure love – free from any bias of ego. David Mutchler has rightly said, "Ego blocks the expression of pure love that flows naturally from Spirit, just as clouds can block light that flows naturally from the sun. Remove the clouds and you have pure sunshine; remove ego and you

> have pure love." He writes further that the ego love is always selfish because it is conditional. But spiritual love is kind and forgiving, understanding and wise, helpful and earnest, genuine and respectful, gentle and honest, gracious and amiable, courteous and fair. Once we are free from ego, this kind of pure love flows automatically and naturally.

To sum up, we can say that our spiritual journey from materialistic consciousness to Spiritual Consciousness or from ego consciousness to Spiritual Consciousness brings first certain internal changes and gives growing awareness of Spirit. It would be difficult to enumerate all such changes for two reasons: First, the list is long; and second, the changes are unique in each individual. But, it is a fact that changes are there in all individuals. All are leading to love, peace, and harmony. And the merit part of this journey is that there is no side or negative effect. By and large, many become less critical and judgemental, and more open to others. They also become more energetic and less prone to worries and anxieties. Growing in spirit is, however, a gradual process. Even a small change takes a lot of time and patience. Therefore, without bothering for the amount of changes, we simply need to move on and on. This is the only way to reach our immediate goal – love, peace, and harmony; or the ultimate goal – merging with God.

REFERENCES

Mutchler, David (2012). *Beyond the Ego.* Bloomington, IN: Balboa Press.

Prophet, Elizabeth C. (2010). *The Story of Your Soul.* New Delhi: Good Times Books.

Wahiduddin, R. S. *Wedding of Body and Soul.* http://wahiduddin.net/purpose/wedding_3.htm

Wahiduddin, R. S. *Taming the Ego ...with the Power of Love.* http://wahiduddin.net/views/taming.htm

Index